Writing Public Policy

*A Practical Guide to Communicating
in the Policy Making Process*

FIFTH EDITION

Catherine F. Smith

New York Oxford
OXFORD UNIVERSITY PRESS

Oxford University Press is a department of the University of Oxford. It furthers
University's objective of excellence in research, scholarship, and education by
worldwide. Oxford is a registered trademark of Oxford University Press in the
certain other countries.

Published in the United States of America by Oxford University Press
198 Madison Avenue, New York, NY 10016, United States of America.

For titles covered by Section 112 of the US Higher Education
Opportunity Act, please visit www.oup.com/us/he for the
latest information about pricing and alternate formats.

Library of Congress Cataloging-in-Publication Data
Names: Smith, Catherine F. (Catherine Findley), 1942- author.
Title: Writing public policy : a practical guide to communicating in the
    policy making process / Catherine F. Smith.
Description: Fifth edition. | New York, New York : Oxford University Press,
    [2018] | Includes bibliographical references and index.
Identifiers: LCCN 2018015552 (print) | LCCN 2018017064 (ebook) | ISBN
    9780190854249 (ebook) | ISBN 9780190854232 (Paperback)
Subjects: LCSH: Communication in public administration. | Written
    communication. | Public policy. | Public administration.
Classification: LCC JF1525.C59 (ebook) | LCC JF1525.C59 S64 2018 (print) |
    DDC 320.6—dc23
LC record available at https://lccn.loc.gov/2018015552

9 8 7 6 5 4 3

Printed by Marquis, Inc., Canada

For John, Ian, Lauren

Brief Contents

Contents

Practices

Conclusion   **Ethics for Policy Communicators**   199

Preface

"In public policy work, if you can't write it or say it, you can't do it." That's how a public policy student summarized the lesson she learned from her internship in a Washington, DC, think tank. She's right. Her observation provides the rationale for this guide.

What Is This Book's Purpose?

This guide aims to develop the know-how, skill, and critical thinking needed for communicating in public policy work. Know-how means understanding the policy process, communication situations, and powers of language. Skill means competence. Critical thinking means discernment or reasonable, reflective consideration of what to believe or do (Ennis). You need all three as a policy communicator. Know-how tells you what to do, when, and why. Skill tells you how. Critical thinking makes you aware of choices.

To support those aims, this guide:

- describes communication as integral to public policy making processes
- identifies communication's functions and limitations
- illustrates typical policy communication contexts, situations, and strategies
- explains standards and expectations for communication in the public sector
- teaches customary policy communication practices and types
- shows examples
- explicates strengths and weaknesses of examples
- considers communication ethics.

Who Is the Intended Audience?

Primarily, this book addresses advanced undergraduate and graduate students in policy-interested disciplines. Entry-level policy professionals will find the guide useful. Active citizens might find it useful, too.

The guide takes a practitioner's viewpoint. It is intended to show students what to expect and what to do as policy professionals communicating in policy workplaces.

What Is This Book About?

This guide's subject is formal written communication in policy making. Guidance focuses on document types that are customarily used in governmental and nonprofit organizational policy making. Goals of the guidance are to make communication visible in the policymaking process and to prepare communicators for varied situations. The current edition recognizes the influence of political discourse on policy making. Policy communication is language use embedded in politics (Stone; Wagenaar). This guide's users are encouraged to think critically about politics as an influential element of policy communication. Critical thinking gives communicators more choice and better control (Lakoff; Luntz; Schon).

Why Is This Book Needed?

Public policy making is demanding work. Communication can be difficult, frustrating work in the hectic conditions of policy workplaces.

Guidance is especially needed now as the culture of policy communication is changing. Technological changes including automated algorithmic analysis of large datasets ("big" data), increased access to government data ("open government"), and robotic communication ("bots") have made policy communication ambiguous. Such large-scale changes cannot be addressed in a compact practical guide. However, cultural changes such as extreme populism, radical conservatism, anti-government advocacy, eroded confidence in governance, and corporate influences on governance are addressed. They are not new, but their influence on political discourse and policy making procedure is both wide and deep, presently. They make the policy communicator's job harder. One experienced communicator says that the job "in today's highly partisan environment is like working near the mouth of a volcano. The challenge is doing your job well without falling in" (Helfert, p. 11).

Most relevant for communication are the changes in values regarding truth telling. Suppression of fact, hostility to objective verification, and deliberate deception are now common in governance. This edition of *Writing Public Policy* addresses these changes in several ways. For know-how, the role of interpretation and the influence of perspective are emphasized. For skill, a code of practical ethics for policy communicators is proposed. Critical thinking is illustrated throughout.

Special Features of *Writing Public Policy*

- illustrations and scenarios from policy workplaces and writers' experiences
- writing samples by professionals, students, and citizens
- commentary on the writing samples
- a general method for communicating in policy work, with checklists of expected qualities for planning, producing, and assessing documents
- specific instruction for selected document types
- demonstration of techniques for writing clearly

Every illustration, scenario, and sample is taken from actual policy work. Most represent the work of professionals in government or nonprofit organizations; some represent the work of students in classroom simulations of policy activity; a few represent both. Students who, at the time of writing, were government professionals or organization interns produced communications in coursework that crossed over into actual use in a policy process. It is important to note that all the samples are examples, not models. They are actual policy work products, presented as written and not edited. Because of space limitations, most samples are condensed. Deletions are indicated by the typographic symbol for ellipsis (. . .). Information on accessing the full sample is provided.

How Is the Book Organized?

Scenarios, writing samples, and illustrative situations provide a realistic and multifaceted view of policy communication without oversimplifying. This immersion approach to developing know-how and skill assumes that broad exposure develops a feel for the territory and a sense of its predictability as well as variability. Consequently, you will not find a singular case of policy making that anchors the instruction. Instead, you will find exemplification and writing samples drawn from multiple real-world legislative and administrative processes. If you find this organization disorienting or confusing, you are experiencing the world of policy making as policy actors do until they get the hang of it.

To make the guidance more usable, aids for using and learning are increased in the current edition. As before, topics such as food safety and military health care continue across chapters like themes in a novel. Exemplars or authors of writing samples appear in several chapters like characters in a novel. They show a policy actor repurposing information according to different audiences or different phases in a policy process. Structural cues such as subheadings, bulleted lists, and templates like the "How To" task outlines in many chapters make concepts easier to grasp initially, to use initially, and refer to later. Overviews, takeaways, discussion topics, and exercises have been added to most chapters. The Introduction describes ways to filter the guidance according to your interests, needs, or time limitations.

What Is New in the Fifth Edition?

- more teaching and learning aids
- more on writing, less on policy
- new sample (Chapter 8)
- more instructive commentary on writing samples
- more on critical thinking and discourse analysis
- proposed code of ethics for public policy communicators (Conclusion)

Limitations

Limits of this guide should be noted. First, it applies to practice; it does not engage theory. While it is informed by academic theory of workplace and professional communication, written composition, discourse studies, and public policy studies, academic concepts are not developed. They are applied to practices of communication in the public sector.

Second, this is not a conventional textbook. It is a guide and a manual of practice. It provides frameworks, methods, tips, and examples from real-world policy work while leaving room for academic teachers and students, as well as nonacademic trainers and trainees, to adapt its instruction to their situations. As noted previously, instructional features are added in the current edition. Chapter references serve not only as source citations but also as recommended readings. A final list of Suggested Reading highlights the best sources for in-depth follow up.

Third, this guide is about governance. It focuses on everyday communication to conduct institutional democracy. A focus on government is justified because government makes most public policy. Additionally, many people know too little about what government does and does not do. Only U.S. domestic policy communication is considered.

This guide is selective in other ways, too. It omits familiar policy communication document types such as press releases in order to teach less familiar types such as witness testimony and formal written public comment. It considers email while it omits social media. (For social media in policy writing, excellent help is available elsewhere, for instance in David L. Helfert's *Political Communication in Action*.) Finally, *Writing Public Policy* is intentionally compact. Some extensive types of policy documentation cannot be adequately addressed in a compact guide. Nonetheless, the instruction applies broadly to communication situations encountered in policy workplaces.

Acknowledgments

This book results from my thirty-plus years as a communications teacher and trainer working with professionals and executives in federal and state government agencies, with advanced undergraduate and graduate writing students at three universities, and with elected and appointed officials in local government. Those practitioners' suggestions, advice, or writing samples are found throughout this guide. Although contributors might not agree with the lessons I draw from their experience, I believe they endorse the aims of this guide and hope they will forgive inadvertent errors.

In summary, I thank continuing contributors (former) Orange County (North Carolina) Commissioner Margaret W. Brown; Penns Valley (Pennsylvania) Conservation Association board members; (former) Pennsylvania Association for Sustainable Agriculture executive director Brian Snyder; National Sustainable Agriculture Coalition policy director Ferd Hoefner; (former) policy director of the U.S. Department of Transportation's National Highway Traffic Safety Administration Carl E. Nash; Marion K. Hook, City of Tucson; Tom Driscoll and Michael Slattery, National Farmers Union, and David Bullock, Research Triangle Institute (North Carolina).

I thank student contributors Elizabeth Graves and Felicia Feinerman (Syracuse University); Ashley O'Neill and Michael Cavanagh (East Carolina University); Gary Redding (University of the District of Columbia David A. Clarke School of Law).

For academic content and critique, I thank William D. Coplin, Carol Dwyer, Frank Lazarski, Stephen Thorley, and Frederick Gale (Syracuse University); Krista Perreira, Daniel Gitterman, Lucy S. Gorham, and Jessica L. Dorrance (University of North Carolina at Chapel Hill); David L. Helfert (George Mason University and the LBJ School of Public Affairs, University of Texas at Austin). For critique from an active citizen's perspective, I thank Susan Warner-Mills, Jinx Crouch, and Suzanne D. LaLonde.

For the fifth edition, Natasha Cooper, Michael J. Pasqualoni, and Peter Wilcoxen, Syracuse University, reviewed and updated Chapter 5 and the Appendix. Kirk St. Amant, Louisiana Tech University, facilitated student review of chapter drafts. David L. Helfert provided a prepublication draft of his forthcoming guide to political communication.

Special thanks to Carl E. Nash and John B. Smith. True friends of this guide, they keep it focused and honest.

Oxford University Press reviewers are silent partners for each new edition. The fifth edition's reviewers were:

- Michael Hayes, Rutgers University–Camden
- Michael D. Jones, Oregon State University
- Hongtao Yi, The Ohio State University
- Two anonymous reviewers

Editors Jennifer Carpenter, Andrew Blitzer, and Christian Arsenault brought forth the fifth edition. Former acquisitions editor Tony English first liked the idea and signed the project for the Press.

References

Ennis, Robert H. (2002). A super-streamlined conception of critical thinking. http://faculty.education.illinois.edu/rhennis/SSConcCTApr3.html

Fischer, Frank. (2003). *Reframing public policy: Discursive politics and deliberative practices*. New York: Oxford Scholarship Online. www.OxfordScholarship.com

Helfert, David L. (2017). *Political communication in action: From theory to practice*. Boulder, CO: Lynne Rienner Publishers.

Lakoff, George. (2014). *The all new Don't think of an elephant!: Know your values and frame the debate*. White River Junction, VT: Chelsea Green Publishers.

Luntz, Frank. (2008). *Words that work: It's not what you say, it's what people hear*. New York: Hyperion.

Schon, Donald C. (1983). *The reflective practitioner: How professionals think in action*. London: Temple Smith.

Stone, D. (2012). *Policy paradox: The art of political decision making* (3rd ed.). New York, NY: W. W. Norton.

Wagenaar, H. (2001). *Meaning in action: Interpretation and dialogue in policy analysis*. Armonk, NY: Sharpe.

Introduction

You will find this book useful if

- you are majoring in the social sciences or humanities to prepare for a career in politics, government, public relations, law, public policy, journalism, social work, or public health
- you are (or might in the future be) an intern in government, in a think tank, or in a nongovernmental organization concerned with public affairs
- you are preparing to enter (or you are already practicing in) a publicly regulated industry or business
- you have (or seek) a job as a communications aide in government or a political action organization
- you have (or seek) a job as a public policy/public relations director in a nonprofit organization or as a public affairs liaison in a corporation, trade organization, professional association, or community service agency
- you are a writer, and you write about public affairs
- you are concerned about a local, national, or world problem, and you want to do something about it
- you want to or are asked to comment publicly on a controversy and you do not feel you have the authority or knowledge or skill to do that.

To benefit from this guide, you do not need prior experience as a student of public policy, as an intern in government, as a student in community-based learning, as an activist in campus or community affairs, or as a volunteer in a nonprofit organization. Any such experience will be very helpful, and you can draw on it often as you use this book. But it is not required. Experience or training in professional or business or administrative communication will be helpful, too, but it is not required.

If you feel intimidated because you don't know enough about your topic of concern or about policy making or about writing, do not worry. Your confidence, knowledge, and skill will grow as you practice the guidance this book offers. (This tip comes to you directly from evaluations by students who used the book.)

How To Use This Guide

Be aware that you bring interests, concerns, willingness to learn, and persistence. Decide on a motivating interest or particular concern. Then, let the guide help you. Use it, do not only read it.

Do you need all of the book or only parts? That depends on your interest, intention, and circumstances. The chapters build on one another, but they can be used separately.

Here's the basic approach to using the guide: First read foundational Chapters 1 and 2. They introduce necessary know-how and skills. In Chapter 2, find a methodical outline of questions to be answered as you plan to communicate. (This Method is professional. It comes to you as the distilled wisdom of many policy professionals who contributed to it.) Use the Method for any policy communication. For a specific communication, answer all its questions to the best of your ability. If you cannot answer some, return to them later when you know more. Use your answers to plan the communication and to revise it. The Method and Checklists in Chapter 2 are your foundation. Start there, and return as often as you need to be confident that you are producing the right communication for the intended purpose, audience, and situation.

Here's a targeted approach: Depending on the specific communication demand, choose the relevant chapter and use its "How To" instructions to compose the document or talk. When you have a first draft, use the Method (Chapter 2) to be confident you have drafted the right communication for the purpose, audience, and situation. To avoid common errors in policy writing and to improve sentence clarity, use tips in the Appendix. To assess the communication's likely effectiveness, use the Checklists (Chapter 2). Finally, revise as needed.

Here's a filtering approach:

- strategically planning a communication? go to Chapter 2 ("General Method")

- writing for different audiences? go to Chapter 2 (Method and Exercise 1)

- writing clear sentences or revising sentences for clarity? go to the Appendix and exercises at the end of Chapters 4 and 5

- ethics? go to the Conclusion

- policy discourse analysis? go to Chapters 1 and 4

- writing samples in a discipline of interest? go to the "List of Writing Samples and Illustrations."

List of Writing Samples and Illustrations

CHAPTER 1

Public Policy Is Language Use

Overview

"In policy work, if you can't write it or say it, you can't do it." You can do it if you know customary policy communication types and you have skills necessary for creating them. And, if you are reflectively, critically aware of your language choices, you can do it better (Schon & Rein). This chapter introduces typical policy communication situations, portrays real-world conditions for communicating in policy workplaces, and critically considers language use by policy communicators. Subsequent chapters help you to develop the necessary writing skills.

* * *

Illustration 1: Milk Labeling

On October 24, 2007, Pennsylvania announced a new standard of food safety aimed to prevent "mislabeling" of food products, especially "misleading" labels. That's public policy, a standing decision by government. An administrative agency, the state's department of agriculture, targeted dairy food as the problem. Under the new standard, milk produced or sold in Pennsylvania could not be labeled "hormone-free." Labels could not say that milk came from cows not treated with "artificial growth hormone" or with "rbGH" or "rbST," common acronyms for recombinant bovine somatotropin growth hormone.

1

Politics influenced this administrative action. Arguably, the agency's decision to target dairy food labeling favored one set of stakeholders, the producer of rbST and dairy farmers who use it. The rbST producer had long argued that saying "no artificial growth hormone" or using similar language on labels harmed sales by implying that milk from cows treated with rbST is unsafe. They cited Federal Drug Administration (FDA) approval for rbST use and scientific evidence of its safety. The state agriculture secretary agreed with this argument.

The agency's decision was immediately controversial in Pennsylvania and elsewhere. News and reaction spread through newspapers, telephone, email, blogs, and chat outlets. Dairy farmers who did not use rbST and who wanted to say so on milk labels rapidly organized to oppose banning "hormone free" on labels. Advocates for sustainable agriculture joined these farmers in support. They countered that the science on rbST's safety is inconclusive, that farmers have a right to inform consumers about their product, and that consumers have the right to make informed choices. Plans for litigation against the state were announced. In parallel opposition, farmers who did use rbST organized to react with advocacy groups in support of the ban. Conflicting values or ideas of public good drove the discourse.

In mid-November, Pennsylvania's governor postponed the ban and then canceled it. On January 17, 2008, the governor, along with the secretary of agriculture, announced two policy changes: a revised standard for dairy product labeling and new procedures for oversight of labeling claims. Under rule revisions, labels are permitted to claim that milk came from cows not treated with rbST, along with a disclaimer regarding its potential for health risk. Dairy food processors are required to verify label claims by having dairy farmers sign affidavits regarding production methods. That's pluralistic, practical policy making in institutional democracy.

This snapshot captures the basics. For a more comprehensive view, read the participants' own communications. They reveal dimensions of debate, and they illustrate a typical mix of policy communication styles. Extracts selected from key participants' statements are presented here. To read the full text of these and related communications, go to the sources cited. The following extracts begin with the state's initial announcement and follow the story as it developed.

Government Chooses a Problem

Memorandum
To: Agriculture and Food Labeling Stakeholders
From: Secretary Dennis C. Wolff
Subject: Product Label Review Update
Date: October 23, 2007

The Pennsylvania Department of Agriculture (PDA) is increasingly being made aware of concerns from consumers, farmers, and public policy makers regarding mislabeled food products. These include concerns as to whether label claims are accurate and verifiable, and whether label claims are misleading.

For example, concerns have been raised that some labels are misleading consumers by promoting what is not in the product . . . I recently called upon help from a group of dietitians, consumer advocates, and food industry representatives on current issues relating to food labeling by establishing the Food Labeling Advisory Committee . . . While widespread food labeling concerns existed, the Committee recommendation is to begin by addressing dairy labeling improprieties. This is a logical starting point, in that the PDA has current legal responsibility to review certain milk and dairy product labels before they are used in commerce.

Local and National Media Disseminate the News and Opinion

"Milk-Labeling and Marketing Integrity"
By Hon. Dennis C. Wolff, Pennsylvania Secretary of Agriculture, *Lancaster Farming,* November 3, 2007

Consumers rely upon the labeling of a product when deciding what to buy for their families. Recently, concern has risen over the way milk products are labeled and the Department of Agriculture has taken action to help consumers make informed decisions about what to buy and to feed their families.

Some labels mislead by promoting what is not in the product, a practice called absence labeling. This marketing strategy is confusing and implies a safe versus not safe product.

. . .

I take issue with the fact that companies use false food labeling tactics to gain a market advantage . . . Ultimately, we are seeking a solution to the labeling issue that will benefit those who produce Pennsylvania's food and those who consume it.

"Consumers Won't Know What They're Missing"

By Andrew Martin, *The Feed,* NYTimes.com, November 11, 2007 http://nytimes.com/2007/11/11/business/11feed.html

The Pennsylvania Department of Agriculture has decided that consumers are too dim to make their own shopping decisions. Agriculture officials in Ohio are contemplating a similar decision. . . .

Dairy Farmers React to Oppose the Ban

Opinion by Todd Rutter, dairy farmer, president of Rutter's Dairy in York, Pennsylvania. *Harrisburg Patriot News,* November 9, 2007. Quoted in Sherry Bunting, "Milk Label Issue Comes to a Boil in Pennsylvania," *Farmshine,* November 16, 2007; reprinted in Consumer Attitudes about Biotechnology, Science & Education, rbST Public Discussion, Penn State Dairy and Animal Science Blogs, *Terry Etherton Blog on Biotechnology.* (http://sites.psu.edu/tetherton/2007/11)

. . . The state's untenable position has only emboldened Rutter's in this regard, prompting us to plan a series of very public activities designed to educate the community and our customers about artificial growth hormones and our strong stance against their use in our milk production, not to mention our right to say so on our labels.

In the next couple of weeks, we will be running full-page newspaper ads, handing out more than 100,000 information cards through Rutter's Farm Stores, posting content at http://rutters.com, and, on Nov. 13, hand-delivering letters to every member of the Pennsylvania General Assembly. Of course, we're also pursuing all legal avenues available to us to protect our right to provide consumer information.

Dairy Farmers React to Support the Ban

Opinion by Daniel Brandt, dairy farmer, Annville, Pennsylvania; PA Holstein Association State Director; Lebanon County Farm Bureau Director, November 17, 2007 at 12:16 pm. Filed under Consumer Attitudes about Biotechnology, Science & Education, rbST Public Discussion, Penn State Dairy and Animal Science Blogs, *Terry Etherton Blog on Biotechnology* (http://sites.psu.edu/tetherton/2007/11/17/rutter-hormonestutter)

In Todd Rutter's little rant in the November 9th *Harrisburg Patriot News*, it is shameful that he had no scientific documents to back up his claims . . . He does nothing to promote milk for what it is and the unprecedented benefits of drinking milk. . . .

Advocates Opposing the Ban Reframe the Debate

"Time to Do the Right Thing with Food Labeling"

Email action alert, November 11, 2007, by Brian Snyder, Executive Director, Pennsylvania Association for Sustainable Agriculture, http://pasafarming .org; Leslie Zuck, Executive Director, Pennsylvania Certified Organic, http://www.paorganic.org; Timothy LaSalle, CEO, The Rodale Institute, http://www.rodaleinstitute.org

On its face, the recent decision by the Pennsylvania Department of Agriculture to conduct a crackdown on what it considers to be false or misleading claims on dairy product labels may seem to be in everyone's best interest . . . The essential question to ask is "What's really in everyone's best interest over the long term?" . . . The whole labeling controversy itself is only a sideshow to the real issues involved here, which have more to do with ethics and the industry-perceived need for the use of performance-enhancing drugs in livestock production . . . The use of artificial growth hormones (rBST or rBGH) is certainly not the only example of such drugs being used on farms today. In fact, the majority of antibiotics sold in America are actually used in livestock production as growth promoting agents, not as treatment for disease in humans or animals as many uninformed, potentially confused consumers might assume.

. . . By all means, it makes perfect sense to employ the "precautionary principle" when research on any aspect of food production is not conclusive—in doing so, the countries of Canada, Australia, New Zealand, Japan, and all 25 members of the European Union have already banned the use of rBST/rBHG in the production of milk.

So what's so wrong if an individual farmer or group of them working together wishes to advertise, even on a label, the choice made not to use such drugs at all, or at least not unless clinically indicated? While we are so busy debating when and how it is proper to put an absence claim on food labels, when do we get to consider the value of being completely forthcoming with consumers and letting them make informed choices?

(Action alert text can be found at https://writetofarm.com/2014/12/08/ let-a-farm-be-a-farm/#more-230)

Expert Comments

"rBST Certified Milk: A Story of Smoke and Mirrors"

By Terry Etherton, Distinguished Professor of Animal Nutrition and Head of the Department of Dairy and Animal Science, The Pennsylvania State University, October 3, 2006 at 4:23 pm. Filed under Agricultural Biotechnology, The Food System, rbST Public Discussion Penn State Dairy and Animal Science Blogs, *Terry Etherton Blog on Biotechnology.* http://sites.psu.edu/tetherton/2006/10/03/rbst-certified-free-milk-a-storyof-smoke-and-mirrors/

The Boston Globe ran a story on Sept. 25th on the decision by H. P. Hood and Dean Foods to switch New England milk processing plants to "rbST-free" milk. In this story, a spokesperson for Dean Foods said, "Even though conventional milk is completely safe and . . . recombinant bovine somatotropin (rbST) is completely safe, some people don't feel comfortable with it" . . . There's little doubt that consumers who have no understanding are easily gulled by such labels . . . "If the future of our industry is based on marketing tactics that try to sway consumers with 'good milk' versus 'bad milk' messages, we are all in trouble," Kevin Holloway, President of Monsanto Dairy, told a group of dairy producers at a September 13th meeting in Washington D.C. . . .

The reality I have observed is that it is easy to scare the public in a 30-second media message. It is impossible to give them a sound scientific understanding about the benefits of biotechnology in the barnyard in 30 seconds . . . One can ask, who wins? Junk science by a knockout. . . .

Government Revises the Policy

"Governor Rendell says Consumers Can Have Greater Confidence in Milk Labels"

Office of the Governor, Commonwealth of Pennsylvania, Press Release, November 17, 2007

Governor Edward G. Rendell today announced that labels informing customers the milk they intend to buy is produced without rBST . . . can continue to be used . . . under new guidelines for accountability. "The public has a right to complete information about how the milk they buy is produced," said Governor Rendell.

Government Promulgates a New Ruling

William Chirdon, Bureau Director, Commonwealth of Pennsylvania, Department of Agriculture, Bureau of Food Safety and Laboratory Services.

"Dear Fluid Milk Permit Holder . . . PDA has received a great deal of input on the standards set forth [in October 2007] . . . Enclosed please find a new document titled 'Revised Standards and Procedure for the Approval of Proposed Labeling of Fluid Milk' dated January 17, 2008 . . . Please review this document carefully and govern yourself accordingly. . . ."

From the revised standard:

"7. Label Representations.

(A) No labeling may be false or misleading. . . .

  i. In no instance shall any label state or imply that milk from cows not treated with recombinant bovine somatotropin (rBST, rbST, RBST, or rbst) differs in composition from milk products made with milk from treated cows. . . .

  ii. No labeling may contain references such as 'No Hormones, Hormone Free. . . .'

  iii. References such as 'No rBST,' 'rBST Free,' 'Free of rBST,' 'No added rBST' may be considered misleading labeling based upon the entirety of the particular label under review. By way of guidance, a label containing such references may be approved if such references are part of language defined in paragraph 7(B) as a 'Claim,' and is accompanied as set forth in paragraph 7(B) by a 'Disclaimer.' An example of such a Claim and Disclaimer would be 'No rBST was used on cows producing this milk. No significant difference has been shown between milk derived from rBST-treated and non-rBST-treated cows.' In such cases, the reference 'No rBST,' or the other references listed above, may be accentuated by different type style or size but not more than twice the size of the other Milk Labeling Standards 2.0.1.17.08 language in the Claim and Disclaimer. . . .

(B) Permitted Claims. The following claims are permitted:

  (i) RBST (referenced to FDA February 10, 1994 Guidance on the Voluntary Labeling of Milk. . . .)

    1. 'From cows not treated with rBST. No significant difference has been found between milk derived from rBST-treated and non-rBST treated cows' or a substantial equivalent. Hereinafter, the first sentence shall be referred to as the

'Claim' and the second sentence shall be referred to as the 'Disclaimer. . . .'"

. . .

PA Department of Agriculture Standards 2.0.1.17.08 (January 17, 2008).

Advocates Opposing the Ban Reflect on the Outcome

"A Day for Celebration and Humility"
By Brian Snyder, Pennsylvania Association for Sustainable Agriculture. Email, January 1, 2008

This is truly a cause for celebration for all of us, especially those who responded to our alerts by sending letters and emails or making phone calls to Governor Rendell's office and the Pennsylvania Department of Agriculture . . . This is also a day for reflection and humility. There were many farmers on both sides of this issue right from the start, and the damage done to the agricultural community in Pennsylvania will take some time to heal. . . . Yesterday's announcement preserved the right of farmers to communicate with eaters about the way food is being produced in a straightforward way. If you think about it, this is just about as fundamental as it gets.

News Media Reports Ongoing Advocacy Supporting the Ban

"Fighting on a Battlefield the Size of a Postage Stamp"
By Andrew Martin, *The Feed*, NYTimes.com, March 9, 2009. http://nytimes.com/2008/03/09/business/09feed.html

A new advocacy group closely tied to Monsanto has started a counteroffensive to stop the proliferation of milk that comes from cows that aren't treated with synthetic bovine growth hormone. The group, called American Farmers for the Advancement and Conservation of Technology, or Afact, says it is a grass-roots organization that came together to defend members' right to use recombinant bovine somatotropin, also known as rBST or rBGH. . . .

National News Media Reports Continuing Debate

"'Hormone-Free' Milk Spurs Labeling Debate"

Christian Science Monitor, April 21, 2008. http://csmonitor.com/
Environment/2008/0421/p13s01-sten.html

Ohio, Missouri, Kansas, Indiana, and Michigan all have pending legislation or rule changes that would limit labeling claims about hormones . . . Some say Monsanto is behind attempts to remove mentions of hormones. "Clearly what's going on is Monsanto is trying to get states to thwart the market from working," says Michael Hansen, senior scientist for Consumers Union . . . But Monsanto contends that milk from cows treated with [its rBST product called] Posilac is safe . . . Monsanto has unsuccessfully petitioned the Federal Trade Commission for a rule change about what it says is deceptive labeling. Other legal action taken by the company and lobbying by farm bureaus to block such labeling has largely failed. Legal precedent appears to uphold the free-speech interest of dairies and the consumer's right to know. . . . As other new agricultural technology reaches the market, labeling debates appear likely to increase, industry analysts say. For example, milk made from cloned animals and their offspring, approved January 15, 2008 by the FDA, has already prompted one labeling bill in California . . . "This [milk labeling] issue will not go away," says the Consumer Union's Mr. Hansen.

▬▶ WHAT THIS ILLUSTRATION SHOWS. At least four policy problems can be defined around milk labeling: (1) agricultural biotechnology; (2) food safety; (3) free speech; and (4) fair trade. The problems are not mutually exclusive. That's typical. Policy problems are often multi-faceted. More important for policy making, a problem cannot be addressed until it is defined for policy purposes. Problem definition requires making language choices. "There are many modes of defining problems in policy discourse, and each mode is like a language people use to express and defend their interpretations" (Stone, p. 14). Language is not neutral or transparent; words bring built-in associations. In a new context, words immediately create new associations. The agriculture secretary's communication uses techniques of framing, narrative, metaphor, and synecdoche to represent both built-in and new associations (Illustration 1, this chapter).

A *frame* is a preconception, a predetermined value, a mindset, or any given condition that affects characterization or definition. Frames influence the definition of a societal concern as a policy problem. Framing selectively emphasizes aspects of the concern, ignoring others, and connects the selected aspects with a selected context or contexts. As a simple example, the color red on a wall in a crime scene photograph might be interpreted as representing blood, paint, ink, lighting, or something else. Your frame or preconception of what happened in the scene will influence your interpretation of red in the photograph. The food labeling concern in Illustration 1 is framed in two different ways according to the communicator's viewpoint. The agriculture secretary uses a market frame to pinpoint labeling as the problem; the sustainable farming advocate uses a health frame to pinpoint rbST use as the problem. Different frames generate different problem definitions and point to different solutions.

The policy actors writing these samples use *narrative* to describe or characterize the problem. Each actor's description of the problem has a storyline. The agriculture secretary's story says the problem of labeling came to his attention through "widespread concerns." In his story, "consumers, farmers, and public policy makers" are potential victims saved by his agency's heroic action. Oddly, his story has a hero, victims, but no villain. He does not say what caused the "widespread concerns" except dairy farmers with their "labeling improprieties." To a critical thinker, that raises a flag. Can victims also be villains? The secretary has previously identified farmers as victims, and now he says they have caused the problem. To a critical reader, that is blaming the victim. Vague cause and unsupported blame call for closer reading. A storyline that clearly identifies victims and heroes but hedges on villains demands scrutiny. In this instance, critical reading would justify skepticism. According to news reports sampled in Illustration 1, the labeling matter did not come to the Pennsylvania agriculture secretary's attention through consumer complaints. Rather, Pennsylvania was approached by rbST's producer, Monsanto, in a multi-state strategy asking states to change labeling regulation to prohibit "absence labeling." Turns out, the concerns motivating the agriculture agency's action were mainly the rbST producer's.

In contrast to the secretary's narrowly focused market frame, the sustainable agriculture organization spokesperson's health frame points beyond milk-labeling to a bigger back story. The back story is the increasing use of chemicals in farming, including rbST, without due consideration of the impacts on animal and human health. For him, this back story is what's missing from the market frame.

When the secretary says "dairy labeling improprieties" motivate his agency's action he is using *synecdoche*, or selective referral to one part of a problem to represent the whole problem. We all use synecdoche to simplify or make quick reference to a large topic, as when we refer to a current federal administration as "the White House. " However, synecdoche can be problematic, an ethical slippery slope, when it over-simplifies deceptively. In Illustration 1, for instance, dairy farmers might reasonably ask why they were singled out for attention. Why not vegetable or meat farmers too? The answer is that rbST is used only in dairy production, and the manufacturer of rbST wanted regulatory protection. Thus, the agriculture secretary's synecdoche, using dairy labels to represent a general problem of misleading labels, is oversimplified and deceptively accounts for his interest in changing label regulation.

Metaphor is another common technique of simplification. Metaphor implies likeness between two things by naming one as the other. In Illustration 1, when the dairy science expert characterizes opposition to rbST use as "smoke and mirrors" and when the sustainable agriculture advocate calls the focus on labeling a "side show," they are using metaphor. One characterizes opposition to rbST as insubstantial ("smoke and mirrors") while the other sees labeling as a distraction from more troubling issues ("side show").

These language uses—framing, narrative, synecdoche, and metaphor—are used routinely, often subtly, in conversation and in policy communication. In policy communication, they might be more obvious in opinion statements than in memos or legislation, but they can be found in any policy communication. So, what is the lesson here? Several key points: first, as writer, you choose how you will represent information or ideas. It's better to be aware of your choices, to choose deliberately and reflectively. Second, your primary material is symbolic representation, whether words or numbers or statistics. Symbols make information or ideas meaningful. Consequently, symbolic awareness is an important kind of policy writer's know-how. As policy theorist Deborah Stone remarks," An astute policy actor . . . must understand and be able to analyze how symbols work" (Stone, p. 160).

Illustration 2: Budgeting

The annual state budgeting process takes place over six months with preset deadlines or milestones. Three budget proposals—the governor's, the house's, and the senate's—must culminate in a single adopted budget by July 1, the mandated start of the state's new fiscal year. Budgeting depends on symbols, both words and numbers. What people call the budget is a written document crafted by a policy communicator. In the following scenario a legislator's communications director does the work.

Early January. The governor proposes a budget for the coming year that represents the administration's priorities and politics. Immediately after the governor's press conference to announce the budget proposal, the chairs of the state's house of representatives and senate budget committees comment publicly on the governor's proposal in a flurry of press conferences, newspaper interviews, and radio and television talk show appearances. Steve, the communications director for the senate budget chair, tracks public response.

At the same time, work on budgets begins in both houses of the legislature. The senate budget committee chair brings his personal staff (communications director Steve and an administrative assistant) to a meeting with the senate's permanent ways and means committee. As a majority party senator, the committee chair sets the senate's budget agenda. The permanent committee, with the help of the current committee chair's staff, develops the senate's budget recommendations. At the first meeting in January they review budget history, the state of the economy (current and projected), and the politics of individual budget items. They compile a rough list of priorities for senate budget recommendations. Steve takes notes. Steve and others will refer to his meeting notes to stay on track as the budget process unfolds and interruptions occur.

January and February. After the first meeting, the permanent committee staff fans out to consult with federal and state fiscal experts, as well as with issue specialists in state agencies, government watchdog groups, and advocacy groups. They get more projections for the economy, and they seek external corroboration for their rough list of budget priorities. Steve goes along to all these consultations and takes notes.

Next, the permanent committee staff solicits budget requests internally from senate members, state departments, and state agencies. Staffers meet with the members, departments, and agencies about their requests. They begin an initial breakdown of line items to include in the senate recommendations. As the ways and means committee staff interacts with multiple parties, Steve stays in touch with the staff. Because Steve will compile and edit the final budget document, he needs to stay informed at all stages.

In parallel, Steve maintains daily or weekly contact with editors and reporters of major news media. He develops relationships and educates the press. They, in turn, keep him up to date on budget-relevant news that he passes on to staff. He maintains good contact both internally and externally because he has dual responsibilities to anticipate debate about the senate's recommendations and to present them in a way that will promote their acceptance by government officials and the public.

February and March. The permanent ways and means committee and the budget committee chair's staff hold a second working meeting. The chair attends. They intensely debate priorities and preliminarily decide on key priorities for the senate's budget policy. Steve attends and takes notes.

The house budget committee responds to the governor's proposed budget in March with its proposed priorities. The combined senate staffs analyze it and compare it with the governor's proposal, as well as with the their own developing proposal. Steve attends the meetings and take notes. While keeping up with these internal meetings he continues to track press and public responses to the governor's and the house's proposals.

About now, Steve begins translating the senate's key priorities (decided at the second working meeting) into key messages. These simple statements identify a key issue and the senate's proposed way of using tax dollars to address the issue. They are framed as the senate's budget priorities. Steve chooses their wording carefully. He persuades the chair's and committee senior staff's commitment to emphasize the key messages at every communication opportunity. Steve will also use them in the final senate budget proposal.

March and April. Throughout March, the senate budget committee staff finalizes its recommendations and interacts with the governor's and house committee's staffs. Steve's attention increasingly turns to drafting the budget or the written document that will both present and publicize senate recommendations. He writes preliminary drafts of the chairman's introduction and the executive summary for the document. These sections are especially important. Steve knows that when the lengthy and detailed document is released many people, including the press, will read only the chair's introduction and the executive summary. He strongly emphasizes the key messages in both. He writes (or edits senior staff's) descriptions of major budget categories (health care, education, housing, and so forth) and line items within each category. From his notes taken in budget working meetings, he develops arguments to support proposed dollar figures for existing line items and new initiatives in each category.

In late March, Steve's attention shifts to planning a comprehensive internal and external presentation strategy to be carried out in June. He must prepare for internal debate in the legislature and for negotiation with the governor's office as well as government departments and agencies during the budget approval process in May and June. Externally, the senate's recommendations will be publicized through a news media and public events campaign conducted before, during, and after formal release of the recommendations document in May.

April and early May. Steve revises the budget document based on committee staffers' review of his preliminary draft and edits of their own drafts. He coordinates with news media and advocacy groups regarding a public relations campaign to accompany release of the senate recommendations.

Mid-May. The finished 600-page document representing the senate recommendations is delivered to the printer. While coordinating printing and proofreading, Steve fields inquiries by the press and the public about the soon-to-be-released recommendations. His main attention goes to writing and editing press releases, other public announcements, and the chairman's comments for the senate budget release press conference.

Late May and June. The senate recommendations are released, distributed, and announced. Simultaneously, the planned public relations campaign gets underway. Throughout June, while the senate and house debate the budget and the governor responds to their debates, events all around the state (preplanned jointly by the Steve and advocacy groups) direct public attention to senate priorities and funding proposals during "health-care week" or "education week" or "citizenship assistance week." Meanwhile, back in the senate, Steve puts out daily press releases, follows up phone contacts by the press or the public, and prepares comments for the chair's use in responding to unexpected developments, politically significant news, or budget controversies.

•━• **WHAT THIS ILLUSTRATION SHOWS.** The problem is the need to finance state government operations and public services in the coming year. The process is the annual budgeting cycle. In this illustration, you can see institutional policy making in a flow of actions on a timeline to conduct the process. You also see the dependency of policymaking on communication, which supports the budget process from start to finish.

Looking at the process from the viewpoint of communications director Steve, you begin to see that budgeting, while orderly as a policy cycle, is actually quite messy in practice. Illustration 2 shows the typical density of information, number of writing demands, need to balance competing interests, need to coordinate actors, even the juggling of schedules that characterize a policy process and create the working conditions for communicators. Not shown are the additional, unexpected events that disrupt the process or the competing demands on Steve's time as he directs all communications, not only budget-related ones, for a committee chair.

Steve learned how to do policy communication on the job. Before becoming the communications director for the senate budget committee's chair, Steve taught writing in a university. As he worked through the budget policy process, he learned some important differences between academic writing and public policy communication. Specifically, he learned that productive policy documents will be:

- germane to a topic, a phase of the process, and specific interests
- strategic or fitted to goals and objectives
- oriented to action

- publicly accessible now and in future
- clearly written, and
- ethical.

Takeaway and Look Ahead

Remember the language resources frame, narrative, metaphor, and synecdoche shown in Illustration 1, this chapter. You will encounter them again in this guide. When you are a practicing policy communicator, you will have occasion to use them as a writer or to recognize them in policy documents as a critical reader. You will also have occasion to think about the ethics of language choices (Conclusion).

Remember the depiction of conditions in policy workplace shown in Illustration 2, this chapter. With that depiction in mind, you will better appreciate the benefits of the disciplined and time-saving approach to policy communication offered in Chapter 2.

For Discussion

1. Commentary on Illustration 1 identifies two frames and two storylines in the writing samples. Can you recognize them? Can you identify other frames and storylines in those samples? Do you think it is helpful to critically recognize frames and storylines in a policy communication? If yes, how is it helpful?
2. Commentary on Illustration 2 concludes by specifying benchmarks or expectations for policy communication. In your experience, what are the benchmarks for academic writing? Are they the same as for policy communication, or are they different?

References

Schon, Donald C. & Rein, Martin. (1994). *Frame reflection: Toward resolution of intractable policy controversies.* New York: Basic Books.

Stone, Deborah. (2012). *Policy paradox: The art of political decision making* (3rd ed.). New York: W. W. Norton.

CHAPTER 2

Communicating in Policy Making

Overview

Policy communication requires know-how, practical skills, and critical thinking. To develop know-how, this chapter describes the policy communication culture and identifies customary communication types. It describes readers' information needs and attention habits. To develop practical skills, this chapter provides a reliable method for creating any policy document. Checklists of qualities expected in good policy communications are provided, too. Exercises apply know-how and skill to writing for readers and to writing for different audiences.

* * *

The Policy Communication Culture—Actors, Practices, Functions

Who generates public policy information? Participants in the policy making process do. "Actors," they are commonly called. Actors create and use information in accordance with their roles in the process. As the term is used here, a role is a function or job with specific responsibility in the process.

Interests motivate actors and influence their role performance. Interests are stakes or concerns, which might be organized (collectively held, ready for action) or unorganized (individually held, latent). For example, a trade association or an advocacy group has organized interest, whereas a dispersed, affected population has unorganized interest. Typically, organized interests acting as groups are most influential. However, individuals acting alone can be influential, too.

For all actors, roles and interests might relate in complex ways and lines between them can be unclear. Some ambiguity of interest is normal, as when an elected officeholder represents constituency interests in seeking a particular committee assignment or in proposing legislation. But other ambiguity might be unethical, as when an officeholder communicates false or misleading information. Ethics guidelines and enforcement procedures, internal and external to government, protect the policy making process (Svara). Even better protection comes from consciously ethical actors who aim to do no harm (Appendix, this guide).

Typical actors in public policy processes include the following:

- providers of goods, services, or activities related to the problem
- consumers of goods or services (if organized)
- experts with specialized knowledge
- advocates and lobbyists representing specific interests
- advocates representing the public interest
- officials with power to decide and authority to intervene

For example, in making policy for highway safety, the following actors would be involved:

- automotive and insurance industries as providers of goods, services, or activities
- organizations of automobile drivers as consumers
- specialists in automobile design or analysts of the economics of transportation as experts
- lobbyists for law-enforcement associations as representatives of specific interests
- advocates for accident victims as representatives of the public interest
- members of Congress, cabinet secretaries, or state governors as authorities with power

Whether they write or speak themselves or they authorize others to do it for them, policy actors generate information in relation to their role. Credibility, or the perceived reliability of information, is judged partly on the information source's role in the process. In the auto safety example, automotive industries credibly generate technical information on safety features of vehicles. Insurance industries credibly generate information on the economic consequences of accidents. Consumer groups credibly provide accounts of experience in using automotive products and credibly identify problematic conditions. Specialists in automobile design or materials credibly report results of research on ways to make cars safer. Expert policy analysts might credibly offer advice on policy options, such as regulation of manufacturers versus education of consumers. Advocates and lobbyists might credibly provide germane information about interested or affected groups, propose policy, and argue for or against policy based on group interests. Elected and appointed officials credibly generate the policy instruments, for instance, to reallocate funds, create a new program, or provide more oversight for existing programs.

To glimpse the range of policy actors communicating in their roles, look to professionals inside and outside government.

Professionals Inside Government

Within government, career or consulting professionals generate most of the working information of a policy process. They communicate in roles as, for example, aides to members of a legislature, experts on the staffs of legislative committees, legal counsels to legislative committees and agencies, executive agency administrators, policy analysts, and technical specialists attached to many offices. The budgeting illustration in Chapter 1 shows them at work. To carry out their responsibilities, they might use any of the following document types:

- one-page fact sheets (summaries limited to one page)
- memos (more developed summaries of varying length)
- position papers or white papers (extensive reportage or analysis including evidence)
- legislative concept proposals (outlines of model or idea or strategy for policy, without details)
- legislative histories (reports of government action or inaction, based on government records)
- committee reports (synthesis of committee decision and history of action on a topic)

- speeches (to be delivered by elected or appointed officials)
- testimonies (to be delivered by executives or professionals)

For some inside professionals, communication is the entire job. Communications director Steve in the state budgeting illustration (Chapter 1) is an example. A communications director is a generalist who:

- writes and produces internal documents of many kinds
- writes external public announcements of many kinds
- produces kits of information for news media to use

Other professional communicators in government are specialists. They include:

- speechwriters who draft talks for officials to deliver
- legislation writers who draft bills for deliberation and formulate laws for codification
- debate reporters who produce stenographic transcripts and the published records of deliberation and debate
- webmasters who maintain government Internet functions (websites, social media, "open government" interactions)

Professionals Outside Government

Significant amounts of information used in policy making come from outside government. Experts in universities, industries, policy institutes or think tanks, nonprofit organizations, and businesses contribute to white papers, reports, and witness testimony in governmental hearings. Outside experts and advocates consulted in the budgeting illustration in Chapter 1 are examples. In addition, professionals and managers in publicly regulated industries and businesses might provide needed information. Unlike government employees who may not engage in public debate, outside experts may express opinion in print or online publications. The expert's blog in the milk-labeling illustration in Chapter 1 exemplifies this practice.

For some outside professionals, communication to influence policy is their job. Lobbyists are an example. They are experts in a subject and are employed by organizations to ensure that policy makers have information about the subject that is germane to the interests of the employing organizations and to ensure that policy makers are exposed to the full range of arguments on a given issue. Lobbyists might brief legislators and their staffs, or they might draft legislation for consideration.

Policy analysts are a different example. They may be either inside or outside government. They are experts in using quantitative and qualitative methods to examine problems and options for solving problems. Analysts might advise policy makers on the choice of policy instruments or interpret research results to aid the formulation of policy.

Active Citizens
Ordinary people in daily life inform and influence public policy making when they:

- write or email officials
- provide formal written remarks on their experience relevant to a problem or a policy in response to a call for comment
- testify about effects of a problem or a policy on their life or their livelihood
- conduct letter-writing campaigns, create email lists, and use phone trees
- form a coalition to cooperate in solving a problem
- create a mechanism, such as a lawsuit or a boycott, to force response by institutional authorities
- lobby as a representative of civic organizations, trade associations, professional associations, communities of interest, or constituencies

The milk-labeling illustration in Chapter 1 exhibits citizen participation in several of these ways.

Communication Functions

In the culture of public policy work, communication is not sufficient, but it is necessary. What does communication do?

1. Communication produces useful information. Useful information in a public policy process has four major characteristics: it is relevant, it serves action, it has consequences, and it is publicly accessible.

(i) Communication is relevant: Every phase of a policy process—to describe a problem, to analyze issues, to argue approaches, to decide on intervention—demands information. Only relevant information helps, however. In deciding whether to provide information, always ask (re-ask, if necessary) and answer these questions: To what does this relate? To whom does it matter?

(ii) Communication serves action: In policy work, information makes things happen. In deciding whether and how to inform in a policy process, always ask and answer these questions: How does this help? What or whom does it help? What or whom do I want to help?

(iii) Communication has consequences: A problem, intervention, or implementation affects other concerns in many contexts. Information's effects can be wide-ranging. While you cannot foresee all consequences, you should try. In deciding whether and how to inform in a policy process, always ask and answer these questions: What is likely to happen as a result of this information? What impacts might this information have?

(iv) Communication is publicly accessible: Policy makers are answerable to the people who give them authority. Therefore, information used in public processes must be publicly available. Officially, it is recorded and preserved by government as an authoritative public record. Unofficially, news media of all kinds and people in everyday social interactions distribute information as well. In deciding whether and how to inform a policy process, always ask and answer this question: How will this information be made public?

2. Communication makes information understandable in context. Understandable means readers can interpret the communication meaningfully. In this guide, context means, narrowly, a particular policy process or a phase in that process. Broadly, context can mean almost anything. In this guide, outside a particular process, context includes the communication culture, the political environment, and the current policy discourse regarding a topic. Understandability in context happens when expectations are activated and met. In order for communication to succeed, information presenters and recipients must have similar expectations.

What expectations? The most basic is interaction, or give and take between people. Presenters expect to give information. Audiences expect to receive information. That give and take is harder to achieve than you might think, however. Quirks in the way human brains work, distractions in workplaces, writers' failure to consider readers, readers' judgments—any of these might get in the way.

Utility and credibility are strong expectations, too. In public policy work, communication must be informative, believable, and trustworthy. What matters is not how much you, the writer or speaker, know. Rather, what matters is how much your readers or listeners know after comprehending what you say. Whether they use your information significantly depends on whether they trust it.

Another influential expectation is communication type or genre. Effective communication begins with choosing the right genre. It ends quickly if the wrong choice is made, e.g., a fifty-page analysis is delivered when a one-page briefing memo is expected.

Finally, policy communication is expected to be efficient. Information products must be coherent, concise, and to-the-point. Efficient communication is appreciated in policy making because working conditions demand it. Public policy work is information-overloaded. Especially in government and nonprofit organizations, time is scarce, schedules are nearly impossible, and attention is always fragmented. You learned about this in the budgeting illustration in Chapter 1. Rarely does anybody in a policy workplace have patience for disorganized, wordy documents or talks without obvious and relevant purpose and authority.

In summary, the cultural view shows us that information functions best in a policy context when it meets expectations. It succeeds when it can be comprehended quickly, interpreted as relevant, trusted as accurate, traced to authoritative sources, and used with confidence by its intended readers.

Understanding Readers' Attention Habits, Information Needs, and Situations

How do expectations function in readers' and writers' minds? Here is a quick sketch of how readers experience reading a document. The sketch applies equally well to listening to a talk such as an oral briefing.

Readers' attention is dynamic, skipping around and making inferences. Readers form quick impressions of the information and its presenter. Readers infer all of the following: the subject (both explicit and implicit), its purpose (both explicit and implicit), who is presenting it, what motivates it, what its point is, and, most importantly, whether it matters. In other words, readers don't just passively consume your words on a page; they actively engage the text, interpret it, perceive what it means. This perception, more than the text itself, is the basis of their understanding. What readers think and feel affects their comprehension. When you hear a reader or listener say "As I understand what you are saying . . ." pay attention. They are telling you how they reconstruct your meaning, rightly or wrongly.

Moreover, readers evaluate or judge the perceived information and its source. For instance, they judge the presenter to be competent in the subject and caring about the reader's time and interest, or not. If they judge that the writer is not knowledgeable or caring, readers turn off. If they have a choice, they choose whether it's worth their time to continue reading (or listening). If they continue, they choose how they will proceed. Typical strategies are to skim all, or to dip in and out, or to read selectively, perhaps only the summary. Readers' criteria are functional, based on the relevance of information to their needs.

Now, here is a sketch of the other side of the experience. This sketch shows you, the presenter (writer or speaker), working with some typical constraints on communicating in policy workplaces. You have met them before in the experience of Steve, the communication director writing a budget document (Chapter 1, Illustration 2).

There is a demand for information. You are responding to the demand alone or in a team of people. You (or you and the team) will present the information in a communication. These are your possible working conditions: You might choose the way you will communicate, or you might use a prescribed form. You might have ready access to relevant information, or not. The recipients might be known to you, or not entirely. The recipients' uses for the information might be known to you, or not entirely. Your intentions or purpose or what you want to achieve might be clear to you, or not entirely. You are aware of (or your team agrees on) the perspective you will take, or not entirely. Similarly, you are sure of your position on the topic (and your team agrees with you), or not entirely. You have limited time. You (or you and the team) must decide how to plan and produce the information product in the time available. You know that your product might be the only means by which recipients will know what you think. You know that it must be designed to fit recipients' needs and circumstances, although you can't be sure what that will be for all recipients. You must make a conscious effort to plan and write for multiple recipients, even if they are hypothetical.

How can a writer working under these hectic conditions stay on track and create a product that meets the benchmarks for communicating productively? A fast way is to write I, You, It drafts as suggested in Exercise 1, this chapter. A steady but sure way is to plan before you write. In classical times, policy makers prepared to participate in democratic assemblies by self-questioning to discover relevant information and valid arguments they wanted to deliver. Self-questioning is still a good planning method. So, a comprehensive set of questions or prompts is offered here as a general method for communicating in a policy process. By responding to its prompts before you write, you will bring your background knowledge and awareness into the foreground where you can better control and use them. You will recognize holes in your preparation that must be filled. There will be fewer surprises ahead if you plan as prompted by these questions. (You can also use them after you write to help you revise drafts.)

Where do the questions come from? They represent the distilled wisdom of policy professionals based on their experience. If your writing experience has been mostly academic, you might be surprised by the questions. They assume policy workplace writing conditions, not academic conditions. (If you have professional policy writing experience, add your own prompts to the list.) These questions will be referred to throughout this guide as the General Method. The Method is accompanied by two Checklists of expected qualities that public policy documents or talks should exhibit. Use the Checklists when you want to assess the functionality and quality of a written policy communication.

Now, you might read the Method and Checklists for familiarity. Later, when you have an actual need to communicate, come back to them. Make a habit of using the Method before you write and the Checklists after you write.

Cautions: if you skip some questions, do not omit whole steps in the Method. All the steps are needed to cover the basics. Omitting a step in the preparation wastes time later. If you are producing a document with many contributors like the budget in Chapter 1, remember to consult the other contributors as needed to answer the Method's questions.

General Method

Step 1: Prepare
First, ask questions about the policy process.

Policy

- To what policy action (underway or anticipated) does this communication relate?
- Does a policy already exist?

Problem

- What conditions are problematic?
- What problem do these conditions present?
- How do I define the problem?
- How do others define the problem?

Actors

- Who are the actors?
- What are their roles?
- What are their interests?
- Who else has a significant role or interest in the process?

Politics

- What are the major disagreements or conflicts?
- What are the major agreements or common interests?
- Which actors are most likely to influence the process or the outcome?

Step 2: Plan
Second, ask questions about the communication.

Purpose
- Why is this communication needed?
- What do I want to accomplish?

Message
- What story do I want to tell?
- What is the storyline?
- What is my message?
- How do I frame my message?
- How does my story, my frame, and my message differ from others on the topic?
- What argument will I make to support my message?
- Does my argument ignore or engage other arguments on the topic?

Role
- What is my function in this process?
- What is my interest in the outcome?

Authority
- Whose name will be on the document(s): Mine? Another's? An organization's?
- For whom does the communication speak?

Reception
- Who is (are) the named recipient(s)?
- Who will use the information?
- How do I want the information to be used?
- Will the document(s) be forwarded? Circulated? To whom? Summarized? By whom?

Response and Effect
- What will recipients know after reading the document(s)? What will users of its information do?

- What is likely to happen as a consequence of this communication?

Setting and Situation

- What is the occasion? What is the time for communicating?
- Where, when, and how will this communication be presented?
- Where, when, and how will it be received? Used?

Form and Medium

- Is there a prescribed form, or do I choose?
- What is the appropriate medium for presentation and delivery? A formal written document? A telephone call? An email?

Contents

- What information will support the message?
- Where will a succinct statement of the message be placed?
- How should the contents be arranged to support the message?
- How will the document's design make information easy to find?

Tone and Appearance

- How do I want this communication to sound? What attitude do I want to convey?
- How do I want the document(s) to look? Is a style or layout prescribed, or do I choose how to present the contents?

Document Management

- Who will draft the document? Will there be collaborators?
- Who will review the draft? Who will revise it?

Step 3: Produce

Based on your preparation and planning, write the document. Do it in multiple, separate passes: draft first, review second, and revise third. Do not mix the tasks. Separating those tasks allows you to focus and to manage your time.

The tasks are outlined here. Use this outline to stay on track if you're working alone, or under pressure, or producing a short document. If you're collaborating or team-writing, or if you're creating a multi-document product such as a budget (Illustration 2, Chapter 1), adapt the task outline accordingly.

Draft

- Produce a complete working draft in accordance with your preparation and plan, which are your answers to the Method's questions.

Review

- Compare the draft to the plan. Highlight any differences. Address the differences as needed.
- Get additional review of the draft by others, if advisable.
- Refer to the Checklists (shown next here) to assess the draft's likely usefulness and to highlight needs for revision.

Revise

- Make the changes called for by review.

Two Checklists

Features of Effectiveness. A public policy communication is most likely to be useful if it addresses a specific audience about a specific problem, has a purpose related to a specific policy action, represents authority accurately, uses the appropriate form, and is designed for use. Here are detailed descriptions of those features:

- ☐ It addresses a specific audience about a specific problem: In policy work, time is scarce. Specifying a communication's audience or intended recipient(s) and the subject or problem saves thinking time for writer and reader (or speaker and listener). The information's relevance for the recipient should be made clear.
- ☐ It has a purpose related to a specific policy action: Policy cycles have several phases. Multiple actions and cycles are underway simultaneously. Timing matters. Agendas change. Stuff happens. Therefore, explicitly stating a communication's purpose and relevance to the recipient makes it more likely to get timely attention.

☐ It represents authority accurately and ethically: Policy communications do more than present information; they also represent a type of participation and power. For a policy communication to be taken seriously, to have influence, and to influence rightly, the communicator's role and status—a citizen with an opinion, an expert with an opinion, a spokesperson for a nongovernmental organization, a government official—must be accurately represented. Honesty helps credibility. Dishonesty harms it.

☐ It uses appropriate form and expression: Settings of policy work have their own conventions for communicating. Use the document type, style, and tone of presentation that are expected for the purpose, that accommodate working conditions in the setting of its reception, and that respect all persons who are actors in the process.

☐ It is designed for use: People's attention is easily distracted in settings of policy work. Dense, disorganized text will not be read or heard. Contents must be easy to find and to use. Written documents should chunk information, use subheadings, and organize details in bulleted lists or paragraphs or graphics. Spoken texts should cue listeners' attention with similar devices.

Measures of Excellence. No two communications are exactly alike, but every public policy communication should try to meet criteria for clarity, correctness, conciseness, and credibility. Here are detailed descriptions of those criteria:

☐ Clarity: the communication has a single message that intended recipients can find quickly, understand easily, recognize as relevant, and use.

☐ Correctness: the communication's information is accurate.

☐ Conciseness: the communication presents only necessary information in the fewest words possible, with aids for comprehension.

☐ Credibility: a communication's information can be trusted, traced, and used with confidence.

Takeaway and Look Ahead

Be guided by policy professionals' working knowledge of the process and communication's role. Use the General Method to stay on track, produce under pressure, and be accountable. Getting a communication right for its intended audience is difficult, but satisfying. Know-how presented in this chapter is foundational for getting it right. Problem definition, perhaps the most challenging and consequential task of policy communication, is addressed in Chapter 3, next.

Exercises

Exercise 1: I, You, and It

If you are a student writing a policy memo in an academic course, who is the audience for the memo? As the Method asks, who is the recipient? Is the recipient also the intended audience? Maybe the recipient is an instructor but the intended audience is a hypothetical congressional representative or a client or an intelligent nonspecialist? If the instructor assigning the memo has not been clear about the intended audience, ask who it is. If an audience is designated, ask for details about that kind of reader. (If you are a policy professional, you might skip this exercise or use it as a refresher.)

Here's a simple way of priming yourself to write for readers. Adapted from a technique for developing abstract concepts, it is called I, You, and It (Moffett, pp. 140-148). It helps writers to articulate what they know and care about, what their intended readers know and care about, and what a general audience might know and care about. The approach in a nutshell: First, think of the topic from the viewpoint of self (I), then of a designated other (You), and finally as an undesignated person (It). For instance, describe your home based on you experience (I), as the destination for a friend needing directions (You), and as real estate advertisement (It).

Practice the following exercise until you can intuitively flip perspectives between I, You, and It. Why? The exercise reduces self-absorption, an inevitable byproduct of struggling to write. Flipping perspectives sharpens your awareness of readers and of different readers. This awareness improves your chances of communicating as you intend.

You can do the exercise with only part, not necessarily all, of a communication. Re-drafting an important paragraph or an overview is sufficient to see the differences of self, another, and everybody as audiences.

I Draft. First, write for your eyes only. Treat the topic as you understand it and view it. Do this rapidly, fearlessly, energetically. Forget the benchmarks for now (Illustration 2, Chapter 1). This is a discovery draft to inform you, the writer. It shows you what you know and how you think about the topic.

You Draft. Then, write a second draft addressed to another person. Tell it like they expect to read it. Accommodate their knowledge and viewpoint. Craft content, organization, and expression for the designated reader's information and use.

It Draft. Finally, write a third draft directed to everybody in the policy context who needs the information. Tailor the content to prompt their prior knowledge of the topic, even if you have to guess what that might be. Bring the benchmarks for good policy communication back to mind, and draft to meet them, as best you can.

Tip: Inexperienced writers (or harried professionals) often jump immediately into writing the It draft. That's a mistake. Doing preliminary I and You drafts is far more efficient and productive.

Exercise 2: Recognize a Document's Features of Readability

Use the Method to analyze a policy document's construction as you read it. Use the Method's questions to filter the document. Note where in the document each question is answered. Note any unanswered questions.

Do this when reading a professional writing sample, such as the report by the Congressional Research Service provided next. Only the report summary is shown. At the summary's end, you will find access information for the full report.

After analyzing the report using the Method, compare your analysis with the commentary that follows the report (What This Example Shows). Feel free to disagree with that commentary or supplement it with your own findings. The point of this exercise is to develop your responsiveness as a reader and your know-how as a communication analyst.

The Federal Food Safety System: A Primer

Renee Johnson
Specialist in Agriculture Policy
January 11, 2011
Congressional Research Service
7–5700
www.crs.gov
RS22600
CRS Report for Congress
Prepared for Members and Committees of Congress

Summary

Numerous federal, state, and local agencies share responsibilities for regulating the safety of the U.S. food supply. Federal responsibility for food safety rests primarily with the Food and Drug Administration (FDA) and the U.S. Department of Agriculture (USDA). FDA, an agency of the Department of Health and Human Services, is responsible for ensuring the safety of all domestic and imported food products (except for most meats and poultry). FDA also has oversight of all seafood, fish, and shellfish products. USDA's Food Safety and Inspection Service (FSIS) regulates most meat and poultry and some egg products. State and local food safety authorities collaborate with federal agencies for inspection and other food safety functions, and they regulate retail food establishments.

The combined efforts of the food industry and government regulatory agencies often are credited with making the U.S. food supply among the safest in the world. However, critics view this system as lacking the organization, regulatory tools, and resources to adequately combat food-borne illness—as evidenced by a series of widely publicized food safety problems, including concerns about adulterated food and food ingredient imports, and illnesses linked to various types of fresh product, to peanut products, and to some meat and poultry products. Some critics also note that the organizational complexity of the U.S. food safety system as well as trends in U.S. food markets—for example, increasing imports as a share of U.S. food consumptions, increasing consumption of fresh often unprocessed foods—pose ongoing challenges to ensuring food safety.

The 111th Congress passed comprehensive food safety legislation in December 2010 (FDA Food Safety Modernization Act, P. L. 111–353). Although numerous agencies share responsibility for regulating food safety, this newly enacted legislation focused on foods regulated by FDA and amended FDA's existing structure and authorities, in particular the Federal Food, Drug, and Cosmetic Act (FFDCA, 21 U.S.C. §§ 301 et seq.). This newly enacted law is the largest expansion of FDA's food safety authorities since the 1930s; it does not directly address meat and poultry products under the jurisdiction of USDA. The 112th Congress will likely provide oversight and scrutiny over how the law is implemented, including FDA's coordination with other federal agencies such as USDA and the Department of Homeland Security (DHS).

In addition, some in Congress have long claimed that once FDA's food safety laws were amended and updated, it would be expected that Congress would next turn to amending laws and regulations governing USDA's meat and poultry products. Food safety incidents and concerns regarding USDA-regulated meat and poultry products are similarly well-documented. A series of bills were introduced and debated in the previous few Congresses. These bills may be re-introduced and debated in the 112th Congress.

(The full report can be found at fas.org/sgp/crs/misc/RS22600.pdf

---

►◄ WHAT THIS EXAMPLE SHOWS. In this report summary, the writer's knowledge, perspective, role in the process, awareness of the policy context and situation, and authority are effectively represented for an It audience.

The first paragraph identifies the subject, food supply safety policy, and the public-sector governmental policy actors, federal agencies and their state counterparts. In broad strokes, the writer represents her knowledge of the domain. The second paragraph brings in another actor, the private-sector food industry, before summarizing the consensus viewpoint that federal government and the industry have together achieved a safe U.S. food supply.

Complication of this consensus view immediately follows. Cueing the reader with a "however," the writer introduces the disagreement among actors that challenges the consensus. Challengers point to a problem, foodborne illness, that has exposed gaps in protection of the food supply. The author's perspective is neutral or not disclosed. She represents a topic as an informed reporter, not a partisan.

The third paragraph opens with a sentence introducing the primary actor who matters most and who is also the report's intended recipient, the U.S. Congress. This legislative actor makes policy that agency actors will administer and industry actors will implement. With the primary actor ("who cares?") in strong focus, attention shifts to that actor's concerns ("so what?"). The policy making context is legislative. The situation is transition between two congresses. Again, in broad strokes, the author describes the previous 111th Congress's legislative solution to the problem of foodborne illness. Possible next steps by the 112th Congress are previewed. Thus, the writer specifies the existing policy, an act by the 111th Congress codified into law, as well as the new policy action getting underway, oversight by the 112th Congress as the law's administration and implementation proceed.

The report is tailored to the policy cycle. It is timely for the legislators' purposes, agenda setting and problem recognition at the start of a new session. This fitting of the report to recipients' particular purposes at a particular time shows contextual, situational, and audience awareness.

Other features of the document accommodate recipients' fragmented attention and their need for confidence in the report's accuracy:

- An advance summary tells readers what the report offers.
- In that summary, four short sections (each a paragraph long) begin with a sentence telling the reader that paragraph's main point. Subsequent sentences provide details supporting that point.
- Immediately after its first use in the document, domain-specific vocabulary (e.g., Food and Drug Administration (FDA) is immediately decoded and its role explained. This accommodates an It audience, the general reader. However, a word in the title, "primer," is not explained, presumably on the assumption that it is generally understood. That might be a flawed assumption.
- At the summary's end, citations enable readers to trace the writer's sources used to compose the document.

A good way to recognize the report writer's strategy for informing a general reader is to look at the story the report tells. Policy communications usually tell a story. The CRS report tells a story of agenda setting and problem recognition. As the story opens, government characters are poised to act further on a new law. The characters are governmental legislators, administrators, and staffs, as well as producers of goods, providers of services, consumers, and subject-matter experts. There are no heroes or villains or victims, but a problem has emerged to reveal flaws in the system. Some characters have previously devised a solution to the problem. Will their solution work as intended? Is it sufficient to solve the problem? To learn the answers, stay tuned.

This story helps to move the reader's attention along. It is compactly told in four sequenced paragraphs. The first paragraph, or prologue, sets the scene and introduces the lead actor. The second paragraph introduces supporting actors and the complication, a problem the readers care about and for which the solution is not obvious. The third paragraph examines the current situation. The fourth paragraph leaves the end open, setting the stage for continued action.

References

Moffett, James. (2017; 1981). *Active voice: A writing program across the curriculum* (2nd ed.). Portsmouth, NH: Heineman Boynton Cook.

Svara, J. (2007). *The ethics primer for public administrators in government and nonprofit organizations*. Sudbury MA: Jones & Bartlett.

↤⊃

CHAPTER 3

Definition:
Describe the Problem

Overview

Problem definition is important. Definition requires description. This chapter prepares you to describe a policy problem. A systematic approach (How To Describe a Policy Problem) is introduced. This How To approach is re-used in subsequent chapters. Make a habit of using this task-by-task approach to creating a policy document after, first, planning the communication's purpose, audience, and objectives (General Method, Chapter 2). Writing samples in this chapter illustrate problem description from multiple perspectives and for varied advocacy purposes. A critical reading exercise offers practice in analyzing a problem description.

* * *

Problem definition sets the topics for debate. Definition also predicts solutions. Different definitions lead to different solutions.

Definition is grounded in a particular description of the problem. Any description must answer these questions:

- What are the problematic conditions? What problem do they cause?
- What are the issues for policy?
- What is your concern? What is your intended reader's concern?
- Who else is concerned (on all sides)?

- What are the key disagreements and agreements among those concerned?

- What plausible and realistic solution can you offer? (optional)

The following instructions guide you to conceiving the problem description before you write. First, use the General Method (Chapter 2) to understand the policy context and communication situation. Second, use "How To" instructions given here to make decisions about the specific document. The Method maps the territory; "How To" maps your route. Make a habit of using both before you write, then checking back with them as you proceed.

How to Get a Problem onto the Policy Agenda

Goals: Recognize problematic conditions; describe the policy problem they present; acknowledge your perspective and your advocacy.

Scope: Is the problem individual or collective; local or broader in impact; well known or unrecognized; widely discussed or little considered; past, present, or anticipated?

Strategy: Provide information that supports the objective in language that expresses your advocacy.

Product: A short (one page) or longer (twenty or more pages) problem description in an appropriate document type.

Communication objective: Purposeful, action-oriented problem description.

Do Tasks 1–4 in sequence. Results of each task will be used to perform the next. Note: this task outline assumes that you are a novice in problem definition. It helps you to conceive a societal concern as a policy problem.

Task 1: Describe Problematic Conditions and Identify Interests in the Problem

To increase your awareness of problematic conditions and to recognize diverse interests, proceed in any (or several) of the following ways:

- Work from direct observation of experiences, practices, effects:
  - Note concerns in your (or others') daily routine that make you aware of the problem.

- Sit for an hour in the office of a service provider to observe people affected by the problem and to observe the practices of policy implementers.
- Visit locales affected by the problem to observe impacts.
- Work from subjective constructions:
  - Listen to or read or write stories (actual or imagined) that refer to the problem.
  - List the most problematic conditions from one viewpoint and then list them from a different viewpoint
- Work from unfinished business:
  - Reexamine a neglected need.
  - Revive a former interest.
  - Return to an incomplete project.
- Work from anticipation:
  - Imagine the consequences if things continue as they are.
  - Imagine the consequences if things change as you advocate.
- Work from ignorance:
  - Choose a matter that concerns others (but is unfamiliar to you) that you want to know more about.
- Work from knowledge:
  - Consider the matter technically, informed by your (or others') expertise.
- Work from values:
  - Consider the matter ethically or legally, informed by your (or others') ideals or commitments.

Task 2: Specify the Issues for Policy

An identified problem is not yet fully conceived or actionable until its issues for policy are specified. Issues refer to stakeholders' concerns, political disagreements, and value conflicts. To recognize such issues, you might do the following:

- Think about impacts of the problem. Who or what is affected by it?
- Conceive the problem narrowly and then broadly. Is it local or more widespread?
- Flip the scope: conceive it broadly and then narrowly. Is it widely distributed or concentrated?

- Think about attitudes. How do different stakeholders perceive the problem? What values (ideals, beliefs, assumptions) are expressed in their definitions?

- Think about authority. How do stakeholders want to address the problem? Do they see government action as a solution? Do they agree or disagree on government's role?

Task 3: Offer Solutions (If You Are Proposing a Solution)

If you already have a positive and feasible solution to suggest, do so. Generally, problem descriptions with a proposed solution get more attention (Bardach). If you don't have a proposal, or if you want to counter a proposal, or if you want to create alternatives, stimulate your thinking with any of these approaches:

- Review the problematic conditions with a fresh eye, looking for unnoticed potential solutions.

- Reconsider a tried-but-failed or a known-but-ignored solution to find new potential.

- Look at the problem from a different perspective (a different stakeholder's, for example).

- Assign it to a different governmental level or jurisdiction if government already addresses the problem.

- Consult with nonprofit groups and nongovernmental organizations that are concerned about the problem.

- Consider doing nothing (keep things as they are).

Task 4: Write the Problem Description

Keep your answers to the Method's questions (Chapter 2) in mind as you draft for the policy context and communication situation. Make sure that the document's content answers the basic policy description questions cited at the beginning of this chapter.

Write with self-awareness. To a large degree, problem definition is subjective. One constituency's problem is another's acceptable status quo. Narrow and exclusive problem definition freezes possibility and invites competing solutions. Broad and inclusive definition imagines change and invites solution by cooperation. It is important to be conscious of your values, assumptions, wishes, and fears in order to describe the problem intentionally or oriented toward action you want. In any policy process, there will be multiple, competing definitions of the problem. To gain perspective on your own definition, you might do I, You, and It drafts of the description (Exercise 1, Chapter 2).

Problem descriptions can be presented in varied document types. If the type is prescribed, use that type. If you are free to choose, use a type that fits your audience, purpose, context, and situation. In this chapter (Five Examples), memorandum, report, position statement, brief, and legislation are illustrated. For academic problem descriptions in varied document types, see *CQ Weekly*, *CQ Researcher* online, and *CQ Researcher's Database* available in print (to users of subscribing libraries) or online (by purchase) at http://library.cqpress.com. For journalistic problem descriptions, see opinion sections of national newspapers such as the *New York Times* (http://nytimes.com/), *Los Angeles Times* (http://latimes.com/), *Chicago Sun-Times* (http://suntimes.com/), or *Washington Post* (http://washingtonpost.com).

Five Examples

Problem description is shown here in an advocacy essay, a briefing memo, a federal agency investigative report, and legislation. Scenarios precede the samples to provide context.

Scenario

The chief of patient information in the Surgeon General's Office, U.S. Reserve Armed Forces, is the subject matter expert for clinical policy questions relating to health care eligibility and benefits, records administration, medical readiness, and associated policies and regulations. She conducts analyses to answer questions in her subject areas and she writes policy documents. Regarding health care eligibility, a problematic condition has caught her attention. While doing routine research to answer an eligibility question, she finds that reserve component soldiers are not eligible for many of the medical and dental benefits available to active component soldiers. Senior administrative officers have long been aware of this condition and they know that increased reserve deployments are worsening it. Senior administrators have previously defined the benefits gap as a policy problem and recommended legislative solutions involving changes to the Department of Defense's health program, without success.

In this context of inaction, the analyst has encountered a problem recognized by others but not, until recently, by her.

With permission from her administrative superiors to revisit the problem, she makes the disparity in military health care benefits a focus of her graduate coursework in communication undertaken for continuing professional education. She utilizes an assignment to write a preliminary description of the problem (Example 1) in order to develop her knowledge of problematic conditions and to practice framing the problem for policy action.

Example 1

MEMORANDUM

To: (Primary Audience—Still being determined)

Cc: (Secondary Audience—Still being determined)

From: (Author)

Date: (Date of publication)

Subject: (Expansion of Healthcare Benefits for Reserve Component Service Members)

Overview of the Problem

Three hundred thousand American citizens serve in the Reserve Armed Force (RAF), with the number increasing daily. Even though the Reserved Armed Force has devoted over 60 million man-days to the Global War on Terror, these Reserve Component (RC) Soldiers do not receive the same medical or dental benefits as their Active Component (AC) counterparts. Due to the different lifestyle of a RC Soldier compared to an AC Soldier and to the varying benefits, Reserve Armed Force units are struggling to meet medical readiness goals for worldwide deployments and operations.

Problematic Conditions

Current Operations Tempo: The current operational tempo of the United States military requires both AC and RC units to deploy on regular and frequent rotations. The RAF was established with a 5:1 ratio of training to operational years of service. Currently, most RAF units are barely meeting a 2:1 ratio. The lack of dwell time between deployments requires Soldiers to maintain a much higher level of constant medical readiness.

Lack of Outside Health Insurance/Financial Hardship: While the majority of RAF Soldiers have civilian employment, the percentage with personal health insurance drops to less than 30% of the force. Even though enlistment contracts require Soldiers to maintain their medical readiness, many do not have personal insurance or the financial means to procure healthcare.

Socioeconomic Status: RAF Soldiers have an average annual income that is 50% less than the average Air National Guard service member. While the "Hometown Recruiting" program has reached small communities and rural areas previously untapped for military service, the majority of the resulting force consists of blue-collar or farm-dependent citizens with a lower than average socioeconomic status.

The Problem

Too many RAF Soldiers are not medically ready for deployment or missions.

Impact of the Problem

With the RAF quickly developing into an operational force, the United States depends on its service members to maintain a high state of medical readiness in preparation for worldwide deployments and missions. The lack of consistent healthcare benefits for RC Soldiers results in a national average of 23% Fully Medically Ready (FMR) Soldiers across the RAF. As a result, units are deploying to combat theaters with 10–15% fewer Soldiers than missions require. The resulting holes in coverage in security forces, logistics support, and medical providers in combat theaters are devastating the war fight and endangering the Soldiers that are able to fight, as they do not have the support they require.

Potential Solutions

Maintain Current System: Maintaining the current policy of 90 days of healthcare benefits prior to arrival at mobilization station will alleviate a small portion of the medical and dental issues preventing Soldiers from deploying. The current system balances the cost of healthcare with the cost of "fixing" a Soldier. This system does not allow for the deployment of Soldiers with issues that are treatable, yet require more than 60–90 days for optimum medical care.

Full Coverage for Alert: Soldiers currently receive full healthcare benefits 90 days prior to their arrival at the mobilization station. While this allows for them to receive care for minor illnesses and annual appointments, it does not allow enough time for Soldiers to receive treatment for more serious, yet treatable illnesses, such as hypertension, gum disease, or dental issues requiring dentures. Extending full healthcare coverage to Soldiers immediately upon alert of the unit will allow for the treatment of 95% of all dental issues, and the majority of illnesses which do not otherwise disqualify for worldwide deployment.

Full Coverage throughout Period of Service: Extending full healthcare benefits to RC Soldiers (which would mirror the full Tricare coverage AC Soldiers receive) would allow Soldiers to maintain a healthier life-style through regular medical and dental appointments. The potential gains of preventive medicine would, over time, reduce the cost of re-actionary medicine for RC Soldiers, resulting in higher readiness rates. Additionally, if healthcare costs were covered, Soldiers could be held accountable for their individual medical readiness under statutes of the Uniform Code of Military Justice.

Next Steps

As the country continues to call upon our Reserve Component forces, it is critical that we establish a more thorough and dependable system of providing healthcare to RAF Soldiers. The discrepancy between benefits received by the AC and RC is monumental, despite the valiant service of both components on the battlefield. I challenge concerned citizens, leaders, and politicians to recognize the time and money being lost on professionally trained Soldiers who are unable to deploy due to preventable medical and dental issues. Disagreement with our coun-try's position in the current war is unrelated to the benefits our Sol-diers deserve for their service. Let us take care of the very men and women who are risking their lives for our country on the dangerous frontlines of the Global War on Terror by improving healthcare bene-fits regardless of duty status or military component.

➤ WHAT THIS EXAMPLE SHOWS. Example 1 illustrates an I draft (Exercise 1, Chapter 2). Its content is narrow problem defini-tion focused on a single affected population. It answers some of the required questions (Task 4, this chapter). It identifies problematic conditions, specifies a problem those conditions present, and pro-poses solution options. It makes no recommendations, except (per-haps inadvertently) in the draft memo's subject line. "Expansion of benefits" in the subject line is inconsistent with the "Potential Solu-tions" section of the document, where alternatives are described but not chosen. As a communication type, problem description might appropriately either include or omit recommendations. However, the communication's purpose must be clear. If this document's subject line more accurately said "Healthcare Benefits Disparity Requires Attention" its purpose would be clearer and it would avoid introducing a solution indirectly.

The major weakness of Example 1 is incompleteness. It leaves some basic questions unanswered (Task 4, this chapter). Specifically, it does not identify other interested stakeholders or potential agreements and disagreements among interested parties. Perhaps stakeholders and interests are implied in the final paragraph sub-headed "Next Steps." But that generalized paragraph does not pinpoint actors or their concerns. And, it does not identify steps to be taken. Additionally, the document lacks credibility because it does not name the writer or intended recipients. Explanation for this omission is that no policy action is underway, so the purposes and audiences are not yet known. Nonetheless, because it is incomplete and not accountable, the document is not ready for use in a policy process. It is not an It draft. This I draft is instructive for the writer because she learns what remains to be done. As an example of policy writing, it illustrates the demand for rethinking and rewriting. It demonstrates the iterative nature of policy writing.

To format this communication, the writer, who is a professional in government, appropriately chooses a written memorandum or memo. This is a common workplace genre intended for quick reading, easy understanding, and efficient referencing in meetings. (In colonial America, it was called a memorial, meaning information to be remembered.) Modern memos are organized top down, with an initial overview followed by topical sections, like the inverted pyramid of news articles. This organization and the memo's compact form fit the time, attention, and accountability demands of governmental workplaces.

Unlike a news article with a single headline, a memo has a header or stacked items identifying the communication's who (sender and addressed recipient), what (subject), why (purpose), and when (transmittal date). Additional intended recipients might be specified in a "cc" ("copied on this communication") item placed either in the header or at the document's end. The memo's subject is identified in the "re" ("regarding") line, which serves as the memo's title. Content is chunked into sections with subheadings (like mini-headlines) cueing readers to the particulars covered in each section.

In Example 1, capitalization ("S" in "Soldier," for instance) reflects prescribed style in the writer's workplace and is retained here. Similarly, "critical" meaning "urgently important" reflects the organization's working vocabulary and is retained here.

Scenario

Previously in this guide, you read a Congressional Research Service summary of the 2011 FDA Food Safety Modernization Act (Exercise 2, Chapter 2). That act had a long legislative history. "Pure food" policy originating in the 1930s generated a steady stream of federal legislative and administrative reforms intended to assure the safety of food that Americans consume. Over decades, congressional committees, commissions, and task forces worked with the endorsement of several presidents to create a body of laws, standards, and regulations, as well as federal agencies responsible for administering them. After 2001, the U.S. "War on Terror" added food security or protection against tampering and deliberate contamination to food safety policy.

These precedents focused on food manufacturing and distribution. Food growing and handling on the farm were not addressed except for the initiation of a national system to identify and track meat animals. Opportunity to pull food growing and handling into the food safety net came between 2006 and 2011. At that time, random events, national elections, and political advocacy converged to enable reform. Illness outbreaks attributed to spinach (2006), eggs (2006), and peanuts (2009) renewed public perception of a food safety problem. National elections in 2008 shifted political power to a new majority in the legislature and administration. Citing illness outbreaks attributed to peanut processing, the newly elected president Barack Obama announced the creation of a new inter-agency food safety working group. "We all eat peanut butter, including my daughters. We need to fix this," he said.

Interest advocacy geared up to influence legislative and administrative initiatives. Legislative committees in the House and Senate drafted new bills, held public hearings, requested reports from research and investigative services, and received advocates' advice on bill provisions. Administrative agencies received advocates' petitions for new rules and held hearings to collect public comment. Intense activity in 2009–2010 resulted in the landmark FDA Food Safety Modernization Act passed by the 111th Congress in December 2010 and signed by President Obama in January 2011. Administrative rule making to set standards and create regulations for enforcement of the new law began in 2012 with proposed regulations and a call for public comment. Based on public comment received, the proposals were pulled back. Revised regulations were announced with a call for comment in 2014.

Sample communications in the 2009–2010 legislative process are shown next. Professionals in government or nonprofit organizations wrote these samples. Condensed versions are shown, along with information for accessing entire documents.

Example 2

FDA Has Begun to Take Action to Address Weaknesses in Food Safety Research, but Gaps Remain

GAO-10–182R, May 24, 2010

Additional Materials:

Accessible Text

Contact:

Office of Public Affairs

(202) 512–4800

youngc1@gao.gov

Summary

The United States faces challenges to ensuring food safety. First, imported food makes up a substantial and growing portion of the U.S. food supply, with 60 percent of fresh fruits and vegetables and 80 percent of seafood coming from across our borders. In recent years, there has been an increase in reported outbreaks of foodborne illness associated with both domestic and imported produce. Second, we are increasingly eating foods that are consumed raw and that have often been associated with foodborne illness outbreaks, including leafy greens such as spinach. Finally, shifting demographics means that more of the U.S. population is, and increasingly will be, susceptible to foodborne illnesses. The risk of severe and life-threatening conditions caused by foodborne illnesses is higher for older adults, young children, pregnant women, and immune-compromised individuals.

In January 2007 GAO designated federal oversight of food safety as a high-risk area needing urgent attention and transformation because of the federal government's fragmented oversight of food safety. The Food and Drug Administration (FDA) is responsible for ensuring the safety of roughly 80 percent of the U.S. food supply—virtually all domestic and imported foods except for meat, poultry, and processed egg products— valued at a total of $466 billion annually, as of June 2008. In 2007 the FDA Science Board, an advisory board to the agency, reported that science at FDA suffers from serious deficiencies. In addition, our prior reviews of FDA's food safety programs have identified gaps in scientific information, limiting FDA's ability to oversee food labeling, fresh produce, and dietary supplements. Further, as part of our recent review on the effectiveness of the strategic planning and management efforts of FDA, 67 percent of FDA managers reported, in response to a GAO survey, that updated scientific technologies or other tools would greatly help them to contribute to FDA's goals and responsibilities; however, only 36 percent of managers reported that FDA was making great progress in keeping pace with scientific advances. In written comments responding to our survey, some managers stressed the need to increase and stabilize funding, recruit and retain top scientists, and make decisions on the basis of scientific evidence.

In this context, you asked us to examine ways in which FDA may use science to more effectively support its regulatory work and to inform the public about food content and safety. This report focuses primarily on FDA's (1) progress in addressing selected recommendations identified by the Science Board; (2) incorporation of scientific and risk analysis into its oversight of the accuracy of food labeling, fresh produce, and the safety of dietary supplements; and (3) a new computer screening tool that may improve its efforts to screen imports using a risk-based approach.

FDA has begun to address selected Science Board recommendations. For example, FDA reported in May 2008 that it created the Office of Chief Scientist and, in May 2009, it added more responsibilities to the office to signal a new emphasis on regulatory science. According to the Acting Chief Scientist, his office plans to identify major scientific cross-cutting opportunities across FDA and to collaborate with other government agencies. However, gaps in scientific information have hampered FDA's oversight of food labeling, fresh produce, and dietary supplements. In addition, FDA's new computer tool—PREDICT—is designed to improve its risk-based import screening efforts by analyzing food shipments using criteria that include a product's inherent food safety risk and the importer's violative history, among other things, to estimate each shipment's risk. FDA has developed a draft performance measurement plan for evaluating the effectiveness of this risk-based approach.

(The full report can be found at www.gao.gov/products/GAO-10–182R/.)

►─• WHAT THIS EXAMPLE SHOWS. Example 2 exhibits many of the qualities in public policy communication that this guide advocates (Checklists, Chapter 2).

The Government Accountability Office (GAO) is a respected research, legal, and investigative agency of the Congress. It does not advocate. However, its reports are often cited by advocates and by legislators during policy processes. GAO's reputation as non-partisan lends credibility to its reports. In addition, this report exhibits features of traceability that lead readers to expect its information to be reliable. By stating (in a letter of transmittal not shown here) explicitly for whom the report speaks (GAO) and to whom it is addressed (a committee chairman) and by referring (in the full report) to review of this and prior reports by the agency concerned (FDA), the report is accountable.

The summary's organization anticipates the report's reception and use in hectic policy workplaces. The summary is compact. It is coherent, with transitional markers such as "first . . . second . . . finally." Key information is easy to find, an especially important feature if the content will be condensed for oral briefings or discussed in public hearings. Within paragraphs, the information is ordered top down or in general-to-particular logical order. Opening sentences summarize; following sentences elaborate. The summary's readers can rely on obvious transitions and repeated order of presentation to scan comprehendingly. Information hunter-gatherers can use these features to target their selections (see the filtering options in "How to Use This Guide," Introduction).

The genre is a report. GAO uses formal written reports as the genre for communicating finished results of investigations to the requesting Congress member. Government agencies sometimes also prescribe a house style of document design. GAO style for report summaries is to have three main sections, usually with sub-headings (Why GAO

Did This Study, What GAO Found, and What GAO Recommends).
For unknown reasons, the summary shown here does not use subheadings. If it did, the report's readability would be even better.

Scenario, continued

As they developed a new food safety bill in April 2009, staff members of the House of Representatives Commerce Committee met
with advocates for sustainable agriculture. According to advocacy
group mission statements, sustainable agriculture is farming that
is ecologically sound, community supportive, and economically
viable. Among topics discussed in the April meeting was advocates' objection to a one-size-fits-all approach to safety regardless
of farm size, scale, or type of operation. Committee staff asked
for alternatives to consider. In response, an advocacy group representative wrote a position statement providing a logic for making
exceptions. The statement (extracted) is presented here.

Example 3

A Message to Public Officials on Food Safety
By Brian Snyder, Executive Director Pennsylvania Association for Sustainable Agriculture (PASA) May 22, 2009
   It seems everyone in elected office these days wants to do something
about food safety. . . . As a community of farmers, we must also come to
terms with the fact that harmful pathogens occasionally present in food
can originate on farms in various ways that at times defy easy explanation.
   . . .
   Now let us consider the desire folks in government have to devise a
legislative solution for the problems of food safety. . . . It is the acknowledged job of government to protect us to the extent possible from neg-
ligence and preventable forms of injury and/or death. But it is distinctly
NOT the job of government to attempt to eliminate risk in life altogether,
nor to impose expectations that may impinge unnecessarily on the free
enterprise activities of the citizenry without a clearly understood benefit.
   More than anything else right now, we need some plain talk on the
real issues involving the safety of our food supply. With good science
available on all sides, there is widespread disagreement about what matters most and why any of us should care.

We at PASA believe quite simply that the most important thing anyone can do to reduce risk in the food system is to make it as locally-based as possible. A safe food system is built on trust, and trust is built on actual human relationships. Such relationships are harder to maintain the larger and more diffuse the food system becomes.

Furthermore, we contend that the greatest risks to food safety occur when two systemic factors are combined: a) "food anonymity" and b) geographically broad distribution patterns. The most basic strategies for achieving a safe food supply, therefore, are not only to keep the distribution patterns as local and/or regional as possible, but also to put the farmers' faces back on the food. In an ideal scenario, both strategies would occur. . . . These two factors should be acknowledged as priorities and properly rewarded by the regulatory authorities right up front.

With this in mind, the following three-tiered structure seems both to be the current reality in food production and marketing systems, and a necessary framework for any successful effort to further regulate food safety and security:

1. Farm-direct—This includes farm stands, farmers' markets, community supported agriculture (CSA) programs (e.g., subscription farms) and other innovative strategies where the relationship between individual farmers and consumers is immediate and understood.

2. Identity-preserved—This involves distribution patterns on a regional scale where the farmer and consumer do not necessarily meet, but the identity of the farm is preserved on products all the way through the system, from field to fork.

3. Commodity stream—This represents sales where no direct relationship between farms and consumers exists. The farm identity is vague or lost altogether, sources are aggregated and distribution tends to be widespread, including food exported to other countries.

Taking them one at a time, we believe there should be minimal intervention by the government in regulating practices in the first tier, with respect to private transactions occurring between individual farms and consumers. . . . Problems arising here can quite naturally be traced quickly and addressed effectively without associated threats to any broad segment of the population.

With the second tier, it is most important to understand that the government has a tremendous opportunity to take advantage of the good things currently happening out there. The goodwill and positive business practices of farmers, processors and retailers who are already participating in local and regional food system initiatives are ensuring a significant degree of traceability that should be supported in any way possible.

Let me say this as plainly as possible. The government has every right to set reasonable standards for food quality and safe production practices. Nonetheless, farmers with their names—and reputations—listed on every package of food should have options to work on a voluntary basis with independent, third-party entities of their choosing in meeting such standards. Such partnering entities might include certifiers of organic, sustainable or natural products, farm cooperatives, breed associations and other trade organizations with a direct interest in supporting best management practices on the farms they serve.

The third tier represents the vast majority of food product consumed in this country and almost all that is exported to others. The need here for clearly stated and enforced quality and safety standards is obvious and should be a central priority of any food-related legislative agenda in the immediate future. . . .

The essential element here is not that there is some theoretical distinction between "good" and "bad" farmers. . . . This is also not fundamentally an issue of "big farms" vs. "small farms," though it appears unavoidable that vocal contingents on both sides of that divide will try to make it so.

The most pressing concern right now is that, in the rush to do something productive on the most public aspects of safety and security in the food supply, our public officials might take action that will a) do too little, for fear of offending some of the powerful interests involved, or b) do too much and thereby inflict real damage onto one of the most promising trends in agriculture to come along in at least half a century. . . .

But if we can really get this right, a visionary and "fresh" approach concerning food safety at local, state and federal levels of government might lead to an agricultural renaissance in this country that will do as much for the economic health of our rural communities as it will for the physical health of our people.

(The complete statement can be found at https://writetofarm.com in category Food Safety Modernization. Posted November 11, 2013)

➤ **WHAT THIS EXAMPLE SHOWS.** This statement illustrates broad and inclusive problem definition, as shown by its language. It uses strategies of combining topics and generalizing goals to expand the problem scope, invite solution by cooperation, and envision comprehensive change. Combinations such as "food safety and security" and "growers and processors" expand the scope. "Community of farmers" and "farmers of all stripes" show the potential for cooperation. Parallelism in the structure of sentences such as this one: "Do as much for the economic health of our rural communities as . . . for the physical health of our people" points up the potential for comprehensive change. When characterizing actors in the process, the writer avoids stereotypes such as "agribusiness, large corporations, family farmers." He uses non-polarizing, generic "farmers," instead. Similarly, the writer argues against thinking in simple dichotomies (e.g., "good" and "bad" farmers or "big farms" and "little farms").

Inclusiveness invites actors who disagree to work together. By framing the problem generally and using an approachable, reasonable tone, the statement invites consideration of alternatives or exceptions.

The statement answers all the questions a problem description is expected to answer (Task 4, this chapter.) It specifies causal conditions, the policy problem those conditions present as seen from the definer's perspective, and issues for policy consideration (e.g., risk standards, product traceability, compliance monitoring).

This writer chose the genre of position statement to present the organization's advocacy. The genre is appropriate for addressing mixed audiences of intended and potential readers. Legislative staff members are the intended readers. Potential readers might be in the writer's state-level organization, national partner organizations, and news media.

Organized as an informal opinion essay, the statement's style is "plain talk on the real issues." (See Write for an Intelligent Nonspecialist, Appendix.) At a key point, the statement blends essay and memo genres. To outline the logic for making exemptions, the writer switches from opinion to analysis. A "three-tiered structure" that is "a necessary framework . . . for reform" is enumerated in a list. Listing and numbering distinguish individual items; indenting surrounds the entire list with blank space. All these devices pull readers' attention to the analysis.

This advocacy statement does not make policy recommendations.

Example 4

Food Safety on the Farm: Policy Brief

October 2009

For over twenty years, the National Sustainable Agriculture Coalition (NSAC) has advocated for federal agricultural policies that foster the long-term economic, social, and environmental sustainability of agriculture, natural resources, and rural and urban food systems and communities. NSAC's vision of agriculture is one where a safe, nutritious, and affordable food supply is produced by a legion of family farmers who make a decent living pursuing their trade, while protecting the environment, and contributing to the strength and stability of their communities. NSAC's work has resulted in federal programs that promote small and mid-sized family farms, increase new farming and ranching opportunities, invest in sustainable and organic research, reward conservation excellence, and expand local and regional food systems.

Over the last several years, the rise in major outbreaks of foodborne illnesses has called into question the sufficiency of the U.S. food safety system. Up until now, food safety regulatory oversight has focused mainly on processing, food handling, and manufacturing sectors—areas shown to be of highest risk for foodborne pathogen contamination. However, several food safety bills have been introduced into the 111th Congress that could directly or indirectly affect farms and ranches by expanding these authorities and making some on-farm safety standards mandatory. In addition, in the spring of 2009, the Obama Administration created an inter-agency Food Safety Working Group through which the Food and Drug Administration and U.S. Department of Agriculture are adopting new food safety standards and oversight, including on-farm measures.

While NSAC applauds Congress and the Administration for taking steps to decrease foodborne illnesses by strengthening federal food safety oversight and enforcement, in respect to farms it urges decision-makers to ensure that:

- Measures are risk-based, focus on risk reduction, and are justified by scientific research;
- FDA coordinates with other state and federal agencies and community-based organizations with food safety expertise or pre-existing standards or training programs for standard development and enforcement;
- Standards do not discriminate against, but rather encourage, diversified farming operations and conservation practices;
- Standards are appropriate to the scale of the enterprise;

- Fees of any kind, if they are imposed, are equitable to reflect different scales of production and ability to pay;
- Traceability rules for farmers should not require more than good, basic recordkeeping (one-up, one-down) of all sales;
- Marketing Agreements and Orders are not used to regulate food safety.

NSAC members and food safety experts agree that the responsibility for ensuring that our food is safe is incumbent on all actors in the food supply chain: from farmers, packers, processors, and distributors, to the final consumer. It is our position, however, that proposals proffering one-size-fits-all solutions to food safety fail to acknowledge the diversity of agriculture and are inappropriate and counterproductive courses of action.

(The complete brief can be found at http://sustainableagriculture. net/wp-content/uploads/2008/08/NSAC-Food-Safety-Policy-Brief-October-2009.pdf/.)

––––––––––

➤ WHAT THIS EXAMPLE SHOWS. This policy brief has a two-part structure, an initial summary (presented in this chapter) followed by policy recommendations (presented in Chapter 4).

In the opening paragraph of the summary, the first sentence introduces the advocacy. The second sentence asserts the viewpoint. The third sentence describes the advocate's credibility based on experience and policy accomplishments.

The second paragraph presents the problem description. Its first two sentences specify causal conditions including triggering events, insufficient regulation, and inadequate policy responses. From the advocate's perspective, the problem presented by these conditions is need for policy reform. A bulleted list draws attention to advocated principles for reform. The list concludes with persuasion by asserting the coalition's position in favor of principled reform.

In contrast to the broad and inclusive language of the problem description in Example 3, the language in Example 4 is narrowly targeted. Each item on the principles list precisely identifies an issue (e.g, science-based measurement), a conflict (e.g., uniform standards vs. scale-appropriate standards), or a policy instrument (e.g., Marketing Agreements in lieu of regulation). By stating the list items as complete sentences, not only single-word topic indicators, the writer can also assert advocacy in each item. Although it is targeted, the language in Example 4 does not freeze solution; rather it engages conflict and pointedly advocates.

Scenario, continued

As versions of food supply safety legislation progressed through the House over the summer of 2009, splits developed in the sustainable agriculture community's attitude toward reform. Advocates divided primarily around the logic for exemption from proposed new safety requirements. Some wanted to exempt farms, including those offering value-added products, based on the size of the operation, while others were more interested in protections related to the style and geographic breadth of marketing programs. During deliberations on the companion Senate bill in the fall of 2009 and 2010, an amendment proposed by Montana Democrat Senator (and organic farmer) Jon Tester and North Carolina Democrat Senator Kay Hagan included a solution that would exempt certain producers based on combined considerations of size and geography. In its final form, the Tester-Hagan amendment allowed for limited exemption of operations with less than $500,000 in annual gross revenue and all sales within the state of residence or 275 miles (if out of state), as long as the farm of origin is made clear on a placard or label. The sustainable agriculture community's debate changed in reaction to the amendment. Some advocates argued strongly for this solution but others continued to push for total exemption from federal government scrutiny for all small farms. Opponents argued that state and local public-health standards were sufficient food supply safety guards.

The Tester-Hagan amendment was accepted in the Senate Health, Education, and Labor Force Committee's bill. Later it was incorporated in the enrolled bill passed by both the House and the Senate. Also incorporated were related requirements for the FDA to assist small businesses in complying with the new law. These incorporations respond to advocates' concerns and demonstrate advocacy's influence on legislation. To illustrate that influence, sections of the final bill are shown next.

Example 5

FDA Food Modernization Safety Act (H.R. 2751 ENR.)

Title I: Improving Capacity to Prevent Food Safety Problems

Sec. 102. Registration of Food Facilities

(b) Suspension of registration.

(2) Small entity compliance policy guide.—Not later than 180 days after the issuance of the regulations promulgated under section 415(b)(5) of the Federal Food, Drug, and Cosmetic Act (as added by this section), the Secretary shall issue a small entity compliance guide setting forth in plain language the requirements of such regulations to assist small entities in complying with registration requirements and other activities required under such section.

(c) Clarification of Intent.

(1) Retail food establishment.—The Secretary shall amend the definition of the term "retail food establishment" in section 1.227(b)(11) of title 21, Code of Federal Regulations to clarify that, in determining the primary function of an establishment or a retail food establishment under such section, the sale of food products directly to consumers by such establishment and the sale of food directly to consumers by such retail food establishment include—

(A) the sale of such food products or food directly to consumers by such establishment at a roadside stand or farmers' market where such stand or market is located other than where the food was manufactured or processed;

(B) the sale and distribution of such food through a community supported agriculture program; and

(C) the sale and distribution of such food at any other such direct sales platform as determined by the Secretary.

(2) Definitions.—For purposes of paragraph (1)—

(A) the term "community supported agriculture program" has the same meaning given the term "community supported agriculture (CSA) program" in section 249.2 of title 7, Code of Federal Regulations or any successor legislation; and

(B) the term "consumer" does not include a business.

Sec. 103. Hazard Analysis and Risk-Based Preventive Controls.

(l). Modified Requirements for Qualified Facilities

(1) Qualified Facilities.—

(A) In general.—A facility is a qualified facility for purposes of this subsection if the facility meets the conditions under subparagraph (B) or (C).

(B) Very small business.—A facility is a qualified facility under this sub-paragraph—
. . .

(C) Limited annual monetary value of sales.—

(i) In general.—A facility is a qualified facility under this subparagraph if clause (ii) applies—

(ii) Average annual monetary value.—This clause applies if—

(I) In the 3-years preceding the applicable calendar year . . .

(II) the average monetary value of all food sold by such facility (or the collective average annual monetary value of such food sold by any sub-sidiary or affiliate . . . was less than $500,000 adjusted for inflation."

(The full bill can be found at H.R.2751 FDA Food Safety Modernization Act. https://congress.gov/bill/111th-congress/house-bill/2751/text?overview= closed&r=1)

•—• **WHAT THIS EXAMPLE SHOWS.** The example shows information moving from advocates' position statements and policy briefs into legislation. In this instance, phrases such as "roadside stands" and "farmers markets" went directly into the bill. This example forcefully shows that problems are defined in words and that word choices matter.

Takeaway and Look Ahead

"Symbolic representation is the essence of problem definition in politics," (Stone, p. 137). Symbolic representation includes more than just words, numbers, or statistics. Representation includes intention, frame, perspective, and viewpoint as well as expression. A written document is the bridge between the writer's intended meaning and the reader's interpretation. This chapter emphasizes the importance of writers' reflection or thinking about intention, frame, perspective, and viewpoint that influence choices involved in writing a policy document. Next, Chapter 4 emphasizes the importance, particularly for policy analysts, of thinking about the political discourse surrounding policy action.

Exercise

Critically Read a Problem Description

Find a published problem description. It may be an academic, journalistic, governmental, or policy professional problem description. Apply standards for problem description found in this chapter (questions that problem descriptions must answer), Chapter 2 (Checklists), and the Appendix. Does the description answer basic questions? Is it likely to be useful to the intended audience? Is it clearly written? If any answers are no, suggest ways to improve the description.

References

Bardach, E. (2011). *A practical guide for policy analysis: The eightfold path to more effective problem solving* (4th ed.). Washington, DC: CQ Press.

Stone, D. (2002). *Policy paradox: The art of political decision making* (Rev. ed.). New York, NY: W. W. Norton.

CHAPTER 4

Evaluation: Analyze and Advise

Overview

Defining a problem does not solve it. Analysis of alternative problem definitions and evaluation of potential interventions are required. Critical analysis of political discourse regarding the problem is beneficial, too. In this chapter, a policy analyst illustrates critical thinking to show a political agenda's influence on a problem definition (Illustration). Writing samples show clearly written policy recommendation (Example 1) and policy option representation (Example 2). Commentary highlights features of readability including sentence construction in the examples. An exercise invites you to practice revising your own sentences. For more guidance on concise policy writing, refer to Writing Clearly (Appendix).

* * *

Policy analysis should:

- characterize a problem according to its size, scope, incidence, effects, perceptions of it, and influences on it
- identify policy choices available to address the problem and the criteria for choosing
- identify perspectives and reasoning apparent in the choices made
- show awareness of other perspectives, reasoning, and choices

- specify the basis (type of analysis performed) for selecting any proposed recommendation, projecting the effects for different groups, and identifying factors that will affect its implementation.

Problem definitions often reflect the politics surrounding the problem. Critical analysis of discourse discovers connections between texts and social or cultural contexts based on examination of language use (Fairclough, 1985). By reading (or listening) critically, you recognize how a problem description constructs the meaning it conveys. You recognize influences including political influences on the construction. You might discover failures of transparency such as unstated ideological assumptions, faulty or misleading arguments, and information gaps. You might question the description's ethics. In practical politics, you might find grounds for opposing a description. Or you might find surprising commonalities between your own and others' descriptions. Commonalities can lead to cooperation.

"Policy analysts need to have well-developed critical abilities" in addition to technical abilities and people skills, says one analyst (Mintrom, p. 22). He remarks, "Policy analysts are at their best when they question the proposals being put forward by others, when they take time to discover why problems are being presented in specific ways, what their sources are, and why they have arisen at this time" (pp. 20–21). Such questioning can reveal the frame or conceptualization and the viewpoint on a problem, possibly reflecting an agenda (Fischer, Graumann).

Problem description expresses these discourse features along with the content of problematic conditions, interest, and so forth. To recognize a description's discursive features, analysts look not only at the content. They also look at the language. Whether for your own or other proposals, discourse analysis is fundamental recognition work (Gee, p. 20).

Critical thinking skills for recognizing discourse features of communication are taught throughout this guide. You will find critical thinking tips in tasks specific to each chapter. For instance, in Chapter 2, you prepare to communicate by planning how you will address perspectives other than your own ("General Method," Step 2). In Chapter 3, you reveal perspectives built into problem definitions by describing a problem from different actors' viewpoints (Task 1). Here in Chapter 4, critical thinking and language awareness are illustrated in several ways including a sketch of critical reading experience, an illustration of critical discourse analysis performed by an expert witness in a public hearing, and commentaries that highlight features of professional writing samples exhibiting the writer's critical thought.

Sketch of Critical Reading Experience

Early on in reading a document, you begin to make inferences about the communication situation. You ask yourself, "Who is providing this information? To whom? Why? Why now?" You look analytically at text features, asking, "What is the message? How is it supported? Any gaps?" You question the communication's context, and you infer its strategy. You ask, "To what does this refer? Where is it coming from? What's its story? Why? Why now?" You might notice how you feel about the communication, asking, "Do I believe this? Do I trust it?"

Critical reading or listening to connect a text with its contexts is different from mining it for relevance. When you read or listen critically, you don't simply hunt for information. You probe, reflect, question.

For an actual instance of critical discourse analysis communicated by a policy analyst testifying as an expert witness in a governmental public hearing, read the following illustration. Extracts from the hearing's transcript are provided, along with information on access to the full transcript.

Illustration: Critical Discourse Analysis By an Expert Witness in a Public Hearing

"Agroterrorism, the Threat to America's Breadbasket"
Hearing by the Senate Government Affairs Committee
November 19, 2003

Republican Senator Susan Collins of Maine chaired a hearing on proposed amendments to extend the 2002 Bioterrorism Act to cover agriculture and food industries. In her statement opening the hearing Senator

Collins defines the problem as the vulnerability of the U.S. food supply chain. As evidence, she cites a paper trail of documentation that she says indicates terrorist intentions to attack the supply chain.

Opening Statement by Senator Collins, Committee Chair

". . . Hundreds of pages of U.S. agricultural documents recovered from the al Qaeda caves in Afghanistan early last year are a strong indication that terrorists recognize that our agriculture and food industry provides tempting targets. According to a new RAND Corporation report, which will be released at today's hearing, the industry's size, scope, and productivity, combined with our lack of preparedness, offer a great many points of attack. Among our witnesses today will be the report's author, Dr. Peter Chalk, a noted expert in biowarfare. . . . A CIA report . . . confirmed that the September 11 hijackers expressed interest in crop dusting aircraft. . . . This horrific page is from *The Poisoner's Handbook*, an underground pamphlet published here in the United States that provides detailed instructions on how to make powerful plant, animal, and human poisons from easily obtained ingredients and how to disseminate them. It was found in Afghanistan. . . . Last spring, a Saudi cleric who supports al Qaeda . . . issued a fatwa, a religious ruling, that justified the use of chemical and biological weapons, including weapons that destroy tillage and stock" [Agroterrorism, 2004, transcript pp. 1–2].

Testimony by Peter Chalk, Witness

The second witness, Peter Chalk, is a risk analyst for the research organization Rand Corporation. He authored the Rand report on biological warfare and agriculture cited by the committee chair in her opening statement. His testimony complicates the discourse she has initiated. Chalk makes measured acknowledgement of the validity of claims made by Collins. However, he qualifies the risk. "Now, although vulnerability does not translate to risk and there are few reported actual incidents of terrorists employing biological agents against agriculture, a realistic potential for such a contingency certainly exists" [p. 14]. He applies probabilistic reasoning to control inferences. "The problem is that you can't extrapolate [a single disease outbreak] to the general agricultural industry because the referent . . . experience is not there" [p. 22].

Chalk then draws attention to the constructed nature of the threat to food production by showing its inadequate risk assessment. ". . . I have only come up with two documented cases of the . . . use of biological weapons deliberately as a political strategy against livestock" [p. 31].

Chalk goes on to rank the risk comparatively. "Despite the ease by which agricultural terrorism can be carried out and the potential ramifications . . . I don't think that it is likely to constitute a primary form of terrorist aggression. . . . However, I think [such attacks] could certainly emerge as a favored secondary form of aggression" [p. 17].

Without referring directly to the Rand report that he authored, Chalk effectively disassociates its findings from the paper trail in which Senator Collins places it. By resisting the committee chair's frame for the report, he controls the use of his knowledge, perspective, and position in this public process.

(The hearing transcript can be found at http://gpo.gov/fdsys/pkg/CHRG-108shrg91045/html/CHRG-108shrg91045.htm.)

━• WHAT THIS ILLUSTRATION SHOWS. The committee chair's opening statement shows faulty cause-and effect reasoning and ideological bias (Smith, 2009). For political purposes, it perceives food production as vulnerable to hostile attack by terrorists. As member of the majority political party and committee chair at the time of the hearing, Senator Collins had the authority and power to frame a discussion of food supply safety. In this hearing, she framed it selectively in connection to terror.

Her opening remarks use five symbolic devices—metaphor, synecdoche, narrative, assembled meaning, and recontextualization—to build the terror frame. Metaphor is implied comparison; in the senator's opening statement, food protection is compared to war. "Today, the Governmental Affairs Committee will examine the vulnerability of America's agriculture and food industry to terrorist attacks, what our Nation must do to defend against agroterrorism, and how prepared we are to respond to such an attack. In the war on terrorism, the fields and pastures of America's farmland might seem at first to have nothing in common with the towers of the World Trade Center or our busy seaports. In fact, however, they are merely different manifestations of the same high priority target, the American economy" (transcript, p. 1) Metaphor here is used to persuade. "Leaders declare war on social problems not only to signal their firm determination but also to create public support for increased funding . . . The war metaphor sanctions draconian measures" (Stone, p. 176).

Synecdoche represents a whole by one of its parts. To represent total breakdown starting from small causes, Senator Collins offers a horror story of disease spread by one sick bird. "The 2002 outbreak of exotic Newcastle disease in California led to huge economic losses for poultry farmers and the quarantine of 46,000 square miles." These losses were triggered by "one infected rooster smuggled across the border from Mexico." From this evidence, she offers a hypothesis: "The ease with which terrorists could replicate these events is alarming" (transcript, p. 1)." The hypothesis relies on synecdoche linking single instances with unbounded potential. "Politicians or interest groups deliberately choose one egregious or outlandish incident to represent the universe of cases, then use that example to build support for changing a policy addressed to the larger universe" (Stone, p. 169).

Assembled meaning is meaning by aggregation, or constructed association among items. In Senator Collins' opening statement, the infected rooster in California is grouped with "one infected pig imported from Hong Kong" and "in Britain one batch of infected feed at one farm" (transcript, p. 1). This assembly represents many-to-one reduction that sweeps unlike items into one category. Like all symbols, assembled meanings are not inherent. Rather, they are created to influence interpretation by readers or listeners. Senator Collins purposefully implies a commonality among unlike items. In parts of her opening statement not shown here she groups agricultural aircraft, underground publications, and chemical weapons to imply a terrorist agenda. Each item is given new meaning by association with the others. This recontextualization creates artificial, distorted significance among the items. While recontextualization is inevitable in discourse, distortion is not. Distortion is a choice. For help in understanding the distinction between recontextualizing and distorting, refer to the ethical principles offered in this guide's Conclusion.

Witness Chalk effectively corrects Senator Collins's misleading aggregation of items. His testimony subtly critiques the chair's position and the terror perspective. Politely, he exposes the lack of actual cause-and-effect association while agreeing that a potential terror risk to agriculture might exist. He addresses the potential risk analytically, citing statistical evidence. His testimony and answers to questions—distinguishing between vulnerability and risk, measuring the probability of risk, declining to speculate beyond available evidence—show him critically analyzing the policy discourse. His critique draws attention to the terror perspective, making its influence apparent and showing its limits. Politely and credibly, the witness constructs alternatives. Functionally, he makes room for argument in the debate.

How to Critically Evaluate Policy and Analyze Policy Discourse

Goals: Critically consider alternative problem definitions, noting influential contextual factors shaping their language. Construct alternative policy responses to the problem.

Scope: A bounded universe of problem definitions and policy responses.

Strategy: Critical analysis of problem definitions including their representation in language.

Product: Short or longer written document that can be easily summarized for oral presentation. Length may vary from one to fifty or more pages.

Communication objective: Policy evaluation based on analysis of policy options and political discourse.

(Note: The following task outline assumes that you are prepared to perform or have performed—outside the tasks listed here—appropriate technical analysis. The outline reflects academic policy memo writing.)

Task 1: Identify the Problem and the Interests

- What is the problem? To what is it germane? Who brings it to attention?

- Why has the problem come to attention now? What conditions led to the problem?

- Whose behavior is affected, or whose concerns are relevant? Who will benefit by solutions to the problem? Who will pay? Who will implement policy to solve it?

- What stake does each interested party (affected groups, target beneficiaries, implementers of policy) have in the problem?

- How does each define the problem? What frame, perspective, and viewpoint is expressed in each definition?

- What ideals and values (equity, liberty, efficiency, security, loyalty) or ideologies (vision of how the world is or how it should be) are expressed in each definition?

- What stories, uses of synecdoche, or metaphors are apparent in each definition?

- What conflicts of values or ideologies are evident among the definitions?

- How does politics influence the problem?

Task 2: Specify Alternative Solutions and Relevant Criteria for Evaluating Them

- What are the goals/objectives of a public policy to solve this problem?

- What symbols or stories or metaphors are evident in the representation of goals/objectives?

- What policy instruments might achieve the goals/objectives?

- What are at least two (alternative) policies to meet the need?

- What are the relevant criteria for choosing the best one? How do stakeholders weigh the criteria? How appropriate are the weights? What are the trade-offs among criteria?

- What would be the outcome of each alternative according to criteria you consider relevant?

Task 3: If You are Making a Recommendation, Specify an Alternative and Explain Your Reasoning

- Which policy option or instrument do you recommend? Why is it best? Why are other alternatives worse?

- What is the basis for your recommendation? What type of analysis supports it?

- What symbols or stories are apparent in the expression of your recommendation?

- How will your choice affect stakeholders?

- On what conditions (political, economic, organizational) does successful implementation of your choice depend?

- What are the constraints (political, economic, organizational, ethical) on implementing your choice?

Task 4: Write the Document: Policy Analysis with (or without) Recommendation

Before you write, consider your readiness to communicate. Do you have needed knowledge and awareness? Use the Method (Chapter 2) to consider the communication situation and to plan your communication. Possibly, in order to sort out readers' information needs, write I, You, and It drafts (Exercise I, Chapter 2). After you write, assess the product by using the Checklists of standards (Chapter 2) and tips on writing clearly (Appendix). Revise as needed.

Policy analysis is communicated in varied document types. If a particular type is prescribed, fit it to your intended purpose and audience. Academic courses might prescribe a policy analysis memo, for instance. If you are free to choose, you might use a memo, a brief position statement, or an extensive discussion paper.

You must cite your sources. Use the prescribed citation style if there is one or choose the APA style (http://apastyle.org/learn/faqs/index.aspx). For more help, consult *The Complete Guide to Citing Government Information Resources: A Manual for Social Science and Business Research* (Cheney) available in libraries.

Two Examples

Example 1

Previously you read that a coalition of sustainable agriculture interest groups advocated principles to guide reform (Scenario 2, Example 4, Chapter 3). Here, you will read selected recommendations derived from those principles. (You may wish to review Scenario 2 in Chapter 3 before reading the recommendations here.)

National Sustainable Agriculture Coalition Policy Brief and Recommendations

Food Safety on the Farm
October 2009

Principles and Policy Recommendations
There is no question that our food system needs to be safer. But if proposed food safety legislation and administrative actions are to have the desired effect of reducing pathogen risks and increasing agricultural innovation, long term sustainability, consumer choice, and availability of fresh, high quality produce, they should reflect the following principles and recommendations.

[Principle] I. Measures of safety should be risk-based, focused on risk reduction, and be justified by scientific research.

Proposed regulations and updated [Good Agriculture Practices] GAP guidelines should focus on the highest risk activities. Several areas of concern are highlighted here:

Centralized Processing: Attention should be given to the scale of the food production enterprise and its potential to distribute products to millions of people. In most of the recent outbreaks of food borne illness, the main source of the problem was centralized processing, distribution, and retail distribution, not growing and harvesting.

Centralized processing and distribution means that a single lapse can sicken a large, geographically dispersed set of individuals. Most documented cases of contamination of fresh produce can be traced to processing facilities where the products from multiple farms are commingled. Leafy greens provide an example. The vast majority of "ready to eat" bags of salads, spinaches, lettuces, and lettuce hearts have unique risks associated with them. In the last ten years, 98.5% of all E. coli illnesses originating in California were traced to processed, bagged salad mixes, not to crops harvested as whole heads, bunched greens, or greens that are cooked.

Manure Use: Properly composted manure is an effective and safe fertilizer. A great volume of research has shown that judicious use of composted or aged manure is essential for maintaining the high soil microbial diversity and biological activity that is vital to soil quality. The buffering or exclusionary role of diverse microbial communities in soils richer in organic matter has been shown to accelerate die-off of E. coli 0157 and plant pathogens in soil. New safety guidelines, standards, and marketing agreements need not regulate all forms of manure use, but should focus on uncomposted or improperly composted manure, and biosolids, which pose a greater contamination risk. The food safety measures in the National Organic Program include rules for compost, uncomposted manure and biosolids, and may be used as an example.

Animals of Proven Significant Risk: Food safety guidelines, standards, and marketing agreements should use the term "animals of proven significant risk," instead of referring to all animals or all wildlife when managing risk. Wild animals do not present a significant contamination risk for produce. . . . Unnecessary control or elimination of wildlife could have devastating impacts on the ecosystems surrounding farms. . . . Instead, new guidelines, standards, and marketing agreements should recognize the relative risk posed by cattle. Studies show that cattle are the primary source of E. coli H7:0157 with up to 50% of some herds being contaminated. . . .

Food safety standards should also encourage conservation measures such as perennial forage, buffer strips, and grasses to filter out contamination in overland water flows from livestock feedlots, loafing yards, pastures, and manure storage areas. Emphasis should be placed on halting avenues of contamination between animals and produce fields, including irrigation water contaminated by run-off from feedlots.

Human Transmission: Experts say that "deficient employee training" is the top food safety problem in the food processing industry. If employees are not properly trained to implement food safety measures, and if hygiene standards are not enforced, unadulterated products will be at risk for contamination.

Water Quality: Quality of irrigation and rinsing water is intimately linked with produce contamination. Irrigation water can become contaminated by nearby large-scale livestock operations or by overflows from sewage systems. Contamination of produce can also stem from the water used to wash produce in processing facilities. FDA must set standards at the processing level to keep water baths from spreading microorganisms among different batches of produce.

Policy Recommendations:

- In developing guidelines and standards, the FDA and USDA should target critical [high risk] control points in the food system, including processing and packaging, the nature of the supply chain (e.g., the number of steps between the farmgate and end-consumer) that have been documented to increase risk.

- Target FDA and USDA research funding to the most critical [highest risk] points of risk in the food system for fresh produce and other raw agricultural commodities; in processing plants, on water testing of farms; on testing other vectors including animals, people, and dust; on the impact on risk of conservation and biodiversity measures; and on the environmental and social impact on farming of any proposed new food safety measures.

- Additional research should be conducted into the role of resource conservation and soil improvement practices, such as vegetated buffers, and maintaining high soil biological activity and diversity, in reducing on-farm risks of food-borne pathogens in produce fields.

- Protect wildlife and biodiversity by focusing on animals of significant risk, rather than indiscriminate animal control, as the FDA and the USDA develop produce guidelines, standards, and marketing agreements.

- Focus safety guidelines, standards, and marketing agreements related to manure on biosolids and uncomposted manure, or improperly composted manure.

- Updated Good Agricultural Practices (GAP) should include recommendations for how to select and use water sources and guidance for producers on how to test water quality at specified intervals.

- Standards should encourage conservation practices that promote food safety.

. . .

[Principle] VIII. Marketing Agreements and Orders should not be used to regulate food safety.

Food safety should be treated as a pre-competitive area that is not subject to commercial competition. As such, it should not be regulated through the federal office in charge of "facilitating the strategic marketing of agricultural products in domestic and international markets"—the mission of the USDA's Agricultural Marketing Service. Marketing agreements and orders are industry-driven and do not have in place a democratic or transparent process for the development of standards and metrics that will ultimately impact all producers in the respective sector. . . .

Policy Recommendation:

- Oppose the proposed national Leafy Greens Marketing Agreement.

(The complete brief and all recommendations can be found at http:// sustainableagriculture.net/wp-content/uploads/2008/08/NSAC-Food-Safety-Policy-Brief-October-2009.pdf)

──────────

➤ WHAT THIS EXAMPLE SHOWS. This policy position statement illustrates critical thinking and, with some exceptions, clear writing (Appendix). The recommendations express the perspective of a minority community, a coalition of groups representing sustainable agriculture farmers in the national industry of food growing and handling. The minority perspective advocates sustainable alternatives to the proposals offered by the majority or representatives of conventional agriculture. For instance, the coalition critiques and opposes a proposal made by an agriculture trade association to reform food supply safety by market management.

Dense detail referring to supporting documentation shows knowledge. The coalition's position statement reuses terminology of sustainable agriculture taken from position statements, policy briefs, and legislative language (Examples 2, 3, 4, 5, Chapter 3). This recontextualization or language reuse is credible because information is explained in relation to its new context. The stated position is ethical because it is traceable and accountable.

Recommendations are adapted to the recipient's authority and power to act. This brief is intended for congressional committee members, so recommended actions call for legislative intervention to fund and authorize programs and to oversee administration.

The coalition's position is stated explicitly and argued logically. Logic functions globally in this text to support coherence; it also functions locally to support specific claims. When a writer claims that something is true, the reader expects supporting evidence. To be taken seriously, positional arguments must support their claims. In this example, claims and evidence tightly relate. Here is an instance:

> *Claim:* The vast majority of "ready to eat" bags of salads, spinaches, lettuces, and lettuce hearts have unique risks associated with them. *Support:* In the last ten years, 98.5% of all E. coli illnesses originating in California were traced to processed, bagged salad mixes, not to crops harvested as whole heads, bunched greens, or greens that are cooked.

Presentation in this example has two strengths, coherence of the whole document and clarity of individual sentences. Readers find written text coherent if it motivates them to read carefully and if it lets them know what to expect so that they can read knowledgeably (Williams & Colomb, pp. 107–108).

Multiple devices are used here to motivate and to guide readers. Listing is one. Listing aids memory. First introduced to a list of principles in the summary of the National Sustainable Agriculture Coalition's brief (Example 4, Chapter 3, readers reencounter the principles in that group's recommendations. Each principle, or "old" information, is listed again, followed by "new" information or recommendations based on the principles. The old-to-new pattern within a list framework is repeated for eight principles, each having up to five related recommendations. Because the content is specialized, densely detailed, and filled with key points, readers' attention might falter without strong guidance by the writer. Here, readers are helped to attend carefully and knowledgeably by the listing framework and the recurring old-to-new pattern. Whether they hunt for target content or read the entire document, readers are likely to feel confident that the writer wants them to understand and to care about the subject. Readers trust such writers.

Individual sentences are typically clear in this statement. The sentence is an important feature in its design for communicating. For instance, each principle is stated as a single, complete sentence. Recommendations are also stated in complete sentences. If the sentence is long, its construction is (usually) understandable. Sentences are most clear when the main character is the subject, and the most important action is the verb (Williams & Colomb, p. 9). Other attributes of clarity are exhibited when 1) there are no long introductions at the start of a sentence, 2) there are no interruptions between the subject and verb, and 3) terms that have several meanings are immediately explained as the writer intends. Readability is enhanced by varied sentence length. A short sentence offers relief. The following instance shows a clearly constructed long sentence followed by a short sentence. Underlining is added for emphasis.

> Most documented <u>cases</u> [subject] of contamination of fresh produce <u>can be traced</u> [verb] to processing facilities where the products from multiple farms are commingled. Leafy <u>greens</u> <u>provide</u> an example.

Example 2

This sample was originally written for a think tank as a report of academic research on taxation as social policy. The report examined taxes paid by low-wage workers. At a legislator's request, the report was revised in 2008 as a policy brief with a recommendation intended for policy makers. The recommendations focus on the earned income tax credit (EITC). The 2008 policy brief is sampled here. A further revision including academic source notes is published in a scholarly journal (Gitterman, Gorham, & Dorrance, 2008).

The brief's evaluation of policy options and a recommendation are shown here. Other parts are shown in Chapter 5 (Example 2, legislative history) and Chapter 6 (Example 1, summary and overview).

Expanding the EITC for Single Workers and Couples without Children (*aka* Tax Relief for Low-Wage Workers)

Daniel P. Gitterman, Lucy S. Gorham, Jessica L. Dorrance

A Discussion Paper prepared for the Center on Poverty, Work and Opportunity at the University of North Carolina at Chapel Hill

January 2007

. . .

Analysis and Policy Proposals

Policy options to expand the EITC for (or provide additional tax relief to) childless single and married workers

A number of policy proposals for expansion of the EITC for childless single and married workers have been offered over the past decade . . . The primary motivations behind these proposals have been to: a) improve tax fairness by mitigating the disproportionate level of taxes paid by single low-wage workers, especially after the tax law changes of the last decade which in many cases have increased the regressivity of the tax code; b) increase this group's attachment to the labor market, as earlier expansions of the EITC have proven to do for low-wage workers with children; and c) reduce the likelihood that workers engaging in significant labor market effort will remain in poverty.

In addition, we discuss three other issues that an expanded EITC for childless single and married workers could potentially address: the need to provide stronger incentives for workforce participation for young workers entering the labor market; high health insurance costs; and the importance of helping all low-income workers build savings and other assets.

In this section, we highlight options for expanding the EITC for single and childless workers, each of which addresses a somewhat different purpose and several of which target specific subgroups of EITC recipients. . . . For each option, we describe its purpose, the policy change needed, the estimated budget impact if available, and complementary policy changes that are desirable.

1. EITC Baseline Expansion for Single and Married Childless Couples

The first proposed recommendation with the broadest impact . . . would increase the EITC to 15.3 percent of earnings to provide relief from payroll and other taxes, doubling the current level of 7.65 percent of earnings. According to estimates by the Center for Budget and Policy Priorities (Furman, 2006), these changes would have an additional budget impact of approximately $3 billion and would increase the maximum EITC benefit for single and married childless workers from $399 to $1,236. Fully offsetting payroll taxes requires an EITC pegged at 15.3 percent of earnings.

. . . However, we note that by selecting differing percentage figures for the share of earnings that would qualify and using different phase-in and phase-out thresholds, an almost infinite number of variations of this proposal could be designed resulting in higher or lower EITC benefit levels and a correspondingly higher or lower budget impact.

. . .

2. Increased Work Incentives for Younger Workers

In addition to the increased work incentives provided by the baseline EITC expansion proposed above in (1), a second policy recommendation would further increase the incentives for young workers to participate in the legitimate labor market by lowering the age limit at which workers without children can qualify for the EITC from 25 to 21. We view this proposal as an addition to the baseline expansion proposed in (1), which is of higher priority, but it could be instituted independently . . . No such age requirement applies to workers with children—as long as they are not claimed as a dependent on another taxpayer's return, they may file for the EITC. . . . An analysis of this type of expansion for younger workers offered by Edelman, Holzer, and Offner (2006) includes an estimate of its cost at between $1 billion and $2 billion. . . .

3. Expanding available funds for monthly health insurance premiums or retirement plan contributions

A third policy recommendation would assist any worker eligible for the EITC to address the high costs of health care and/or to increase funds available for retirement plan contributions. The health insurance component is particularly relevant to single and childless workers because they are less likely to qualify for Medicaid or the State Children's Health Insurance Program (SCHIP). Workers could enroll in the Advance EITC, which pays low-wage workers an extra amount in their regular paycheck each month. They would then target that Advance EITC to pay a share of their health insurance premium . . . A similar approach could be used for an employer-based retirement plan, such as a 401(k). As was true for proposal (2) to make childless workers eligible for the EITC beginning at age 21, we view this proposal as working best if it were in addition to a baseline expansion of the EITC since this would increase the funds available for health insurance premiums or retirement contributions.

. . .

4. Helping Childless Workers to Save and Build Assets

. . . Because [the EITC] can represent a significant amount of money to receive in one payment, it is often used by low and moderate-income families as a way to save money over the year. As generations of experience

with traditional welfare has shown, however, a marginal increase in income rarely ends the poverty cycle for a family without some accumulation of assets. Federal policies have long favored the development of assets through tax breaks for 401(k)s, mortgage interest, and small businesses, and initiatives like the GI bill. Unfortunately, most of these policies do not benefit low-income families, who may not earn enough to pay income tax or have access to tax-deferred retirement accounts.
. . .

An expanded EITC for childless workers has great potential to be an essential component of a more far-reaching initiative to reduce poverty and build assets if we are willing to experiment with and invest in innovative approaches. We propose that the matched savings account concept be expanded so that, in this case, single and childless workers could use the added income from an expanded EITC benefit to invest in savings vehicles such as Individual Retirement Accounts (IRAs), Coverdell Education Savings Accounts (ESAs), and college savings 529 accounts and that their contributions be matched.
. . .

Lastly, we consider three complementary policy recommendations that would assist savings and asset building initiatives linked to an expanded EITC. The first is to make the Saver's Credit, which Congress recently made permanent, fully refundable so that it is more advantageous to low-income savers. The second calls for Congress to appropriate funding to the IRS to fund community free tax preparation programs for low-income tax filers similar to the funds it has provided for free tax preparation programs for the elderly and military families. . . .

The third, and final, proposal related to expanding opportunities for asset building, is to increase, or eliminate, the asset limits that are attached to a range of public benefit programs and which have a dampening effect on the propensity of public benefit recipients to save. . . . This issue is of particular concern to workers with disabilities since they often must rely on social security and Medicaid.

Conclusions and Suggestions for Policy Reform Putting an EITC for Singles in a Broader Federal Tax Policy Context
. . .

Distributional and fairness concerns have always emerged during debates on broader tax policy reform proposals. As part of large congressional reconciliation tax-cut packages, EITC expansions have been used to maintain distributional equity for tax policy reform as a whole. . . .

The simple conclusion of our work is that workers without children who live below the poverty line should not be subject to high federal income taxes and taxed deeper into poverty. We hope to begin a dialogue rather than recommend one way to policy reform.

. . .

The most significant challenge for policymakers, policy researchers and Washington DC think tanks concerned about federal tax relief for low-income single and married couples without children is to continue to generate thoughtful empirical analysis and policy conclusions that show how to make our tax code fair for those workers and non-custodial parents who also work hard and play by the rules. The politics of tax policy research will continue to pose major challenges for research on the distributional implications of tax reform. The key challenge is how the trio of federal individual income tax provisions—personal exemptions, standard deduction, and tax credits—together can shelter a certain amount of earned wages from federal tax liability and thus increase the amount of take-home pay of all low-wage workers. Certainly, the budgetary environment of the moment does not hold a great deal of promise for expanded EITC commitments. Yet, recent political history over the last three decades demonstrates that new or expanded work and family support efforts are indeed possible politically, even at times of budget and economic stress. . . . An expanded EITC for single and childless workers could emerge as a proposal with considerable political traction.

(The policy brief can be found at http://law.unc.edu/documents/poverty/publications/gittermanpolicybrief.pdf./)

➤ **What This Example Shows.** This writing sample illustrates the flow of policy analysis between research and practical politics. It demonstrates policy communicators' ability to write for multiple audiences and to communicate a message in multiple communication types. It demonstrates skill in authoritative argumentation to support a recommendation. (See Chapter 6 for an outline of its argument.) The argument exemplifies critical thinking to evaluate policy options, to explore values inherent in the recommended policy instrument, and to identify limitations as well as benefits of utilizing that option. In claiming that tax policy represents political agendas, the brief shows critical analysis of policy discourse. The claim is supported by a legislative history tracing policy changes to power shifts in government over time. You can read its legislative history in Chapter 5.

Takeaway and Look Ahead

Policy analysts recognize that policy proposals are always political on some level. Whether reading analysis or writing it, they recognize that communication represents not only information but also discourse. Accountable communicators expect to persuade by means of well-argued, evidence-based, clearly articulated, and discourse-aware analysis. To inform your persuasion and improve your evidence-using skills, the next chapters focus on government records research (Chapter 5) and policy argumentation (Chapter 6).

For Discussion

If you encounter out-of-context information re-used to make a claim for which there is little or no evidence, how will you respond? Will you dispute it? How will you express your objections? Review the testimony by Peter Chalk (Illustration, this chapter) as you consider your answer to this question.

Exercise

Who's Doing What? Simplify Sentence Construction

Select a paragraph in a policy memo you are writing. Assess the paragraph's clarity and concision. For each sentence in the paragraph, note the length (number of words) and underline its main actor (subject) along with its main action (verb). Mark sentences that have multiple actors (subjects) and actions (verbs). Those probably need revision. Select one of the marked sentences, and revise it to simplify or condense it. Your objective is to rewrite the sentence to answer the question "Who's doing what?" by constructing that sentence around one main actor (subject) and action (verb).

Before you revise, study the following demonstrations.

Original

> In developing guidelines and standards [action #1], the FDA and USDA [actor #1] should target [action #2] critical high risk control points in the food system, including processing and packaging [modifier #1], the nature of the supply chain (e.g. the number of steps between the farmgate and end-consumer)

[modifier #2+], that have been documented to increase risk [action #3]. (59 words)

Revision

FDA and USDA guidelines and standards should target critical control points in the food system. Targets should include documented causes of increased risk such as packaging, processing, and the supply chain (e.g., the number of steps between the farm-gate and the end-consumer). (44 words)

Explanation: Revision breaks the original long sentence into two shorter ones. Each has a single main actor (subject) and action (verb) and says who's doing what. Necessary modifiers are carefully placed near the main actor and action; repetitive modifiers are omitted. For old-to-new continuity between the two sentences, the main action of the first sentence carries over to become the main actor in the next sentence. The revised paragraph is now two well-constructed sentences. The paragraph uses fewer words; it is clearer and more coherent.

Here's another demonstration using the same revision technique with even more impressive results.

Original

Control of aviation noise rests primarily with state and local governments as a result of public law shifting responsibility away from federal government. This has contributed to inconsistencies in aviation noise control and abatement policies across the nation. As a result, major gaps exist in protective coverage of all its citizens from noise pollution. (paragraph: 53 words; sentence length: 15–20 words)

Revision

State and local governments now administer the control of aviation noise pollution. Consequently, control is inconsistent nationwide. Gaps in protection exist.

(paragraph: 21 words; sentence length: 4–12 words)

Explanation: Word count goes down, unnecessary repetition goes away, sentence length varies when each sentence has a main actor, the subject, and action, the verb. While the verb in the revision's second sentence might be stronger for more emphasis, "is" works in the context.

References

Agroterrorism: The threat to America's breadbasket. (2004). A hearing before the committee on governmental affairs, U.S. Senate, 108th Congress, 1st session, November 19, 2003. Washington, DC: U.S. Government Printing Office.

Cheney, D. (2002). *The complete guide to citing government information resources: A manual for social science and business research* (3rd ed.). Bethesda, MD: LexisNexis.

Fairclough, N. (1985). Critical and descriptive goals in discourse analysis. *Journal of Pragmatics*, 9, 739–763.

Fischer, Frank (2003). *Reframing public policy: Discursive politics and deliberative practices.* New York: Oxford Scholarship Online. Oxford-scholarship.com

Gee, J. P. (1999). *An introduction to discourse analysis: Theory and method.* London, England: Routledge.

Gitterman, D. P., Gorham, L. S., & Dorrance, J. L. (2008). *Expanding the EITC for single workers and couples without children: Tax relief for all low-wage workers.* http://law.unc.edu/documents/poverty/publications/gittermanpolicybriefs.pdf

Graumann, C. F. (2002). Explicit and implicit perspectivity. In C. F. Graumann & W. Kallmeyer (eds.), *Perspective and perspectivity in discourse* (pp. 25–39). Amsterdam: John Benjamins.

Mintrom, M. (2012). *Contemporary policy analysis.* New York, NY: Oxford University Press.

Smith, C. F. (2009). Public professional communication in the antiterror age: A discourse analysis. In G. F. Hayhoe & H. M. Grady (eds.), *Connecting people with technology: Issues in professional communication* (pp. 90–117). Amityville, NY: Baywood.

Stone, Deborah. (2012). *Policy paradox: The art of political decision making* (3rd ed.). New York: W. W. Norton

Williams, J. M., & Colomb, G. C. (2012). *Style: The basics of clarity and grace* (4th ed.). Boston, MA: Longman.

CHAPTER *5*

↭

Legislative History: Know the Record

Overview

If you want government to act on a concern, you need to know the history of prior action or inaction on the concern. For that, you need research and reporting skills. This chapter prepares you for government records research and interpretive reporting of legislative history. Examples demonstrate persuasively written interpretation of legislation to show the history of an issue (Example 1) and of a law (Example 2). An exercise offers practice in revising sentences for clarity.

* * *

Many kinds of information are needed for policy making. To frame a problem, identify its issues, or propose interventions, you might need to know about influential social history, technological developments, and economic patterns. You might consult scientific research, public testimony, advice of expert consultants and lobbyists, statistical data, government agency reports, transcripts of legal proceedings, and more. But one kind of information is essential: the history of government action on the problem.

Why is knowledge of the legislative record important? Three reasons. First, precedent matters. Policy builds on prior action. Second, context matters. The record shows deliberation and debate surrounding action. Third, content matters. The preamble or purpose statement of a published bill or law enables you to discern original intent. If you are proposing new action, your credibility as well as standards for policy argument demand that you know the history of prior action.

Who conducts legislative research and for what purposes? Government staff members (and sometimes interns) consult the legislative record to help them frame problems and identify issues. Outside government, professional staff (and sometimes interns) in organizations of many kinds such as nonprofit groups, trade associations, and policy institutes consult the record, as do academic scholars and students. Knowledge of prior action informs their advocacy or analysis. Similarly, citizens consult the record as independent researchers. They might pursue an activist interest or volunteer to conduct research to support an organization or an understaffed local government. Legal action also sometimes requires knowledge of the legislative history. Court clerks, attorneys, law librarians, legal services professionals (and sometimes interns) regularly consult the legislative record to know a law's intent as part of adjudicating disputes over a law's meaning.

Who writes legislative history documents? Often, the people who conduct the research also write the report. Government staff, professional researchers on contract to a committee or agency, or volunteers might produce a legislative history tailored to a particular need to know.

Interns are often assigned legislative research and writing tasks. To illustrate, here's a hypothetical situation, a composite of actual internship experiences. A supervisor in a healthcare policy institute asks an undergraduate intern to specify unmet needs in elder health care for a position paper being written by the institute's director. The internship carries course credit enabled by a formal academic partnership between the institute and the university where the undergraduate is studying toward a degree. The supervisor gives the intern no instructions on how to gather the necessary information. The intern has not previously conducted research in government records or written a legislative history. But she is willing, intellectually curious, and persistent.

She considers how to approach the task. She figures that to identify unmet needs, she must know what current law provides. As a strategy for getting started, she works from familiar experience. Her grandparents experienced nursing home care, so she decides to start by collecting information on nursing homes.

She goes, first, to the institute's reports published on its website. She finds in-house (written by institute personnel), in-depth analyses of individual laws. But, because the website has limited search capability, she cannot find specific references to nursing homes except by reading all the reports. She does not have time for that. She then tries an online search using Google for the term "nursing home care." That yields advertisements for nursing home businesses and websites of advocacy groups focused on specific issues regarding nursing homes, but little legislation or public debate.

Stymied, she asks the institute's professional staff for help. A policy analyst tells her that the institute subscribes to a commercial database of government information relevant for writing federal legislative histories, called ProQuest Legislative Insight (http://proquest.com/products-services/legislativeinsight.html). It supports varied search techniques and has good user instructions. He suggests that she do exploratory searching there. He also makes the time-saving suggestion to keep track of her work by using another of the institute's electronic resources, EndNote (endnote.com). That is a licensed software application for note-taking and government document citation management.

She takes his advice. First, she learns about the capabilities of ProQuest Legislative Insight by looking at the user instructions, especially the "how do I?" tips and the finding aids. She is already familiar with EndNote, having used it previously in academic research.

As she learns more search options, she understands that her initial efforts focused in nursing home care were too narrow. Now she feels ready for a bigger picture of multiple issues relating to elder health care. However, time is tight. To avoid hit-or-miss searching, she pauses to frame a search strategy. She thinks about evidence the institute director might need to argue a position on unmet needs in elder health care. Because she knows the purpose and the user for the research, she is well prepared to filter the data that her searches yield. *Tip:* Before reading further in the intern's story, you should pause to skim the "Fundamentals of Good Research" in "How To Conduct Government Records Research and Write a Legislative History," this chapter.

After learning the chosen database's capabilities, she proceeds. Her confidence in searching grows as she uses the database's filters and finding aids. Filtering by time range and date proves most productive for her purpose. Filtered search results show that a good time to focus on would be the years in office of the previous federal government administration. For an overview of action in that time frame, she looks first for published Congressional Research Service (CRS) (https://fas.org/sgp/crs) legislative histories of individual elder health care laws. Based on the overview, she extends her search to the current administration, selects current laws and proposed bills, and reads them in some detail. She checks the final action taken on each, carefully noting the final action's bibliographic identifier so she can easily return to it if needed.

Late in the day, the thought occurs that she knows little about the debate surrounding any of the actions. While the chosen database provides some contextual materials, which she quickly browses, they are not exactly what she needs. Again thinking creatively about how to fill in the details of debate about particular legislation, she remembers that her university library subscribes to VoxGov (http://www.com), an aggregator of government social media that includes congressional committee hearing transcripts and floor debates. She has access to VoxGov through her university's subscription because her internship is for course credit. So, in the little time remaining for research, she logs in remotely to VoxGov, then browses in order to gain insight as to the politics of elder health care. The intern does this to inform herself; she knows that the institute director is politically well-informed. Because the institute for which she is an intern is not a licensee, she will not include information from VoxGov in her report to the institute director.

By the end of the day, she writes a two-page legislative history of elder care. Her report is not simply a summary of findings. Rather it interprets the record of action and inaction during the last administration to argue for the highest priority needs. To interpret, she makes a judgment based on preliminary research. In the report, she states her basic criteria for identifying the most pressing current needs. The criteria are recognition of a problem and failure to act on it. She specifies problems that were recognized by the previous administration but left unresolved. From the range of bills or amendments proposed but not passed or adopted, she derives a list of unmet needs. This list comes together efficiently from her research notes. The list would not have been possible without the notes. She ranks the needs in order of priority, using refined criteria that refer to concerns revealed in public debate. For each priority, she summarizes essential debate in a sentence. In a concluding reference list, she cites relevant bills or amendments using standard APA citation style (assisted by EndNote) so that the institute director can quickly find them to read their language. Task accomplished.

This hypothetical intern's experience captures fundamentals and good qualities of government records research. Those fundamentals and qualities translate to step-by-step instructions provided next in this chapter. Sample legislative history reports then follow.

How to Conduct Government Records Research and Write a Legislative History

Goal: Knowledge of U.S. proposed or enacted law regarding a defined problem based on consulting legislative records.

Scope: Either a single law or an issue involving multiple laws. Relevant action might be at the federal, state, or municipal level or at several levels. In addition to legislative records, administrative records of rule making and regulation as well as judicial records of litigation might be needed.

Strategy: After deciding on the focus, a law or an issue, apply the fundamentals of good records research.

Product: Written history of either a law or an issue involving multiple laws and, possibly, including administrative rules. Sources are cited using standard government documents citation style.

Communication objective: Credible reporting and interpretation of legislative action.

Fundamentals of Good Research

- *Know why the research is needed.* Knowing the purpose for the research tells you what, and how much, to look for. Will the information be used to make new law (legislative) or to interpret existing law (legal)?

In either case, there might be a published history that meets the purpose. Or you might need to find the records required to write a specialized history. Knowing the purpose for the research can help you (or a librarian assisting you) to decide where to look first. Do you want to find a history or write one?

- *Know the user and the user's purpose for the information.* Who, exactly, will use the information, and what is the interest or need? The user might be you, gathering information for personal use or for an academic or internship assignment. Or the user for whom you are conducting the research might be a legislator who wants to amend an existing law. Knowing the user's purpose tells you what, and how much, to look for. Federal records only? State or municipal records also?

- *Set the scope.* Will the research follow a single law through all its forms and related actions—bill, codified statute, administration, regulation, amendment, and (possibly) adjudication? Or will your research follow an issue through policy changes and across multiple laws over time? What is the relevant time frame? What is the relevant level of government?

- *Take the necessary time and manage your time.* Records research can take hours, days, or weeks, depending on how much you already know, what you are looking for, where the records are, how well you have planned, and other contingencies. Prepare for the reality that legislative records research will take time, probably more time than you initially planned. What is your deadline for completing the research? What is your schedule for conducting the research and writing the necessary documents?

- *Use existing skills and add needed ones.* If you have a well-defined problem, are willing to learn, are curious and persistent, and have basic research skills including the ability to ask questions, identify relevant sources, and search databases, you are basically ready to perform legislative research.

You might need to learn about the legislative process, government record types, and standard or new tools for researching government records. If so, review as necessary using the tools suggested next here.

Task 1: Review the Legislative Process

If you already know federal legislative procedure well or if you are tracing state law, omit Task 1 and go on to Task 2.

As you conduct research in government records, you can feel as if you are drowning in data, classification systems, procedure names, and document types. Especially if you start into records searching without knowing the underlying legislative process, you will quickly become lost. Use the following reviews of the process to revive your effort. Bookmark your favorite and return to it as often as needed to refresh your knowledge:

- The House: "How Our Laws Are Made: A Ghost Writer's View" (by House of Representatives Office of Legislative Counsel), https://legcounsel.house.gov/HOLC/Before_Drafting/Ghost_Writer.html

- The Senate: "Enactment of a Law" (by U.S. Senate Parliamentarian, Robert B. Dove, [Washington: Government Printing Office, 1997]), https://www.senate.gov/legislative/common/briefing/Enactment_law.htm/

- "The Legislative Process" (by U.S. House of Representatives), http://house.gov/content/learn/legislative_process/

- "How Does Congress Work?" (by Indiana University Center on Representative Government), https://corg.indiana.edu/how-does-congress-work

Task 2: Conduct Research

Frequently Asked Questions (FAQ)

Before starting to search, it might be useful to skim these sources for comprehensive tips:

- Congress.gov Frequently Asked Questions (FAQ), http://www.congress.gov/help/faq/ (free)

- Congress.gov, https://congress.gov|Library of Congress (free)

- ProQuest—*Legislative Insight*, http://proquest.libguides.com/legislative insight (by subscription or purchase)

What Do You Want?

Do you want to find a history or write one? Decide early whether your purpose is served by using an already published history or by producing one. For single federal laws, commercial research services such as ProQuest publish legislative histories with varying levels of detail. Free public services such as the Library of Congress also publish legislative histories. To find a published history for a federal law, these are good sources:

- Library of Congress, "Federal Legislative History: Initial Steps," http://loc.gov/law/help/leghist.php/
- Law Librarians' Society of Washington, DC, http://llsdc.org/
  - *Legislative Source Book*
    - Federal Legislative History 101
    - Federal Legislative History Research: A Practitioner's Guide
- ProQuest Legislative Insight: Quick Start LibGuide http://proquest.libguides.com/quick_start_legislative_insight (for use by subscription or purchase)

You are unlikely to find published legislative histories for an issue. Typically, issue histories are produced on demand by or for users who want the information specialized to their purposes. If you are writing an issue history, use the Policy Tracker tool at CQAlmanac (http://library.cqpress.com/cqalmanac) to follow the developments.

Federal, State, Local Records Access

As a general rule, federal records are accessible online and in research libraries. State records are less available. A state's records might be online or, more likely, in the print archives of the state's library. Local government records accessibility varies. Few local governments put all their records online. Ask the government of interest how to access the record. Before you ask, check these state-by-state overviews of state legislature and local government record accessibility:

- State and Local Governments (Library of Congress), http://www.loc.gov/rr/news/stategov/index.html/
- Law Librarians Society of Washington, DC, *Legislative Source Book*: "State Legislatures, State Laws, State Regulations," http://www.llsdc.org/state-legislation

Federal and some state records are available through government information services, either free or by subscription. Free services such as the Library of Congress (http://loc.gov/) can be accessed using any online browser. Subscription services such as ProQuest (http://ProQuest.com/) are accessed by authorized users of facilities provided by research institutes, some for-profit organizations, university libraries, and large public libraries.

Free Access

At home and in many public libraries, you can freely access federal records and link to online state records through the following sites:

- USA.gov: https://www.usa.gov

- Library of Congress: https://www.loc.gov/rr/news/stategov/

- Government Publishing Office: http://www.gpo.gov/fdsys/ (until late 2018)

- Government Publishing Office "Beta" Site: https://www.govinfo .gov (will replace the fdsys GPO site in late 2018)

Free access to numerous federal government websites that link to records is also provided by these academic portals:

- Government Information (Syracuse University Libraries) http:// researchguides.library.syr.edu/government

- Clark Library Government Information Collection (University of Michigan), http://www.lib.umich.edu/clark-library/collections/ government-information/

- Government Documents/Information (Mansfield University), http://mansfield.libguides.com/govdocs/

Academic libraries offer another valuable resource: librarians! They can advise you on what's good, and what's available to you. For professional, skilled, courteous, up-to-date assistance in government records research, ask a librarian.

Record Formats

- Research university libraries and large public libraries have original federal government records in all available formats— digitized, paper, and microfiche. Increasingly but not entirely, all these formats are becoming available online. You should not exclusively rely on online sources, however. Depending on your research objective you might need government records in any or all formats. Some older public records available only on paper or microfiche might be essential for answering your research questions. The point: to assure that you are reaching all the relevant records for your topic and your questions, ask the government documents specialist in a research university library for help.

Notes and Citations

- Take detailed notes as you conduct research. Notes should include but not be limited to bibliographic identifiers or citations for legislation. Citation management software applications can now make both citing and note-taking easier. Recall the hypothetical intern's use of the application EndNote. Many applications are now available by subscription or purchase. *Tip:* Ask a research librarian what applications are available to you.

Make sure to note contextual information about the target record. Note names of people, committees, subcommittees, and bill or law citations mentioned in the target record. Why? If your first search method fails, these notes can restart your search; they give you alternative ways to search. For instance, if the hypothetical intern researching elder health care jots down key subject words, personal names, dates, and citations, she is prepared to search by any of the following filters:

- subjects discussed in the record (for example, "home nursing," "elder health care," "Medicare");

- personal names, dates, committees, or other elements of a legislative process (for example, the names of the senators sponsoring a bill; the popular name of target legislation; the names of witnesses testifying in legislative hearings);

- citations (number and letter "addresses" of a legislative record expressed in a standard citation style such as H.R. 1091–106 for a House of Representatives bill).

Task 3: Write the Legislative History Document

To write your legislative history, begin by using the Method (Chapter 2) to plan the document. Let your intended reader's needs guide content selection. As you draft the document, check your near-final draft against the communication standards (Checklists, Chapter 2). Revise as needed to produce the final draft.

Legislative history writing is interpretive. Even if the report is only a list of significant prior legislation, the list itself represents a selection or interpretation. Think of legislative history as a report of government records research to support a message. The message is your conclusion formed after consulting the record. It is your interpretation of your findings. While the history's scope is set by the purpose (whether you are writing a law history or an issue history) and by the amount of information required, you nonetheless select and organize findings to support a message.

You have several options for organizing the history's contents: chronology (to show developments over time), significance (to highlight influential legislation), trend (to show a pattern), or a combination of these options. Use the organization that best fits the user's need.

If no format is prescribed for presenting the results of your research, you might choose to use the standard reporting format for professional and technical communication:

- An overview that succinctly states the message and key findings,
- Following the overview, subsections of summarized findings,
- Subheadings that descriptively label each subsection according to that section's contents, and
- Citations of record sources following their introduction in each subsection.

Citation

Citation is vital in a legislative history. Credibility, utility, and ethics rely on citing sources. The history's accuracy must be verifiable and the practical needs of the information user (as well as the researcher) demand that all sources be easy to locate for confirmation and referral. Citation is the means to all those ends.

Citation management software applications, if they are available to you, can make citation easier. In any case, as a policy communicator you should understand the elements of government records citation and why each element matters.

Full citation or government style is preferred in legislative history writing, in contrast to terse citation or legal style. If either government style or legal style is prescribed for you, use that style. If not, choose a style and use it exclusively. Do not mix styles.

Full citation provides three kinds of information about a source: what type of record it is, how it is classified in a system of documentation, and who publishes it (a commercial research service or government). By including the publisher of your source, full citation maintains licensing agreements if your source is proprietary.

To inform your know-how, here is a list of the elements in a full citation, or government style:

- Issuing agency (house, number, session, year)
- Title (document number and name; long name may be abbreviated)
- Edition or version
- Imprint (city, publisher, date of publication)
- Series (serial list of publications)
- Source (publisher if print or database if online)
- Medium (online, print, or microfiche)
- Online address (URL)

- Accessed date (in parentheses)
- Notes (in parentheses, add anything not already included in the citation that helps to locate the document or maintains licensing agreements)

Following are two illustrations of government style:

1. U.S. House. 101st Congress, 1st Session (1989). H.R. 1946, A Bill to . . . Authorize the Department of Veterans Affairs (VA) to Provide Home, Respite, and Dental Care. Washington: Government Printing Office, 1990. (GPO Microfiche no. 393, coordinate C13.)

2. U.S. House. 104th Congress. "H.R. 3, A Bill To Control Crime." (Version: 1; Version Date: 2/9/93). Text from: Full Text of Bills. Available from: ProQuest Congressional; Accessed: 7/04/05.

In the second illustration, the source is a proprietary database available only to licensed subscribers.

If you need more help with citation, especially if you are a student researcher who is not a law student, consult these sources:

- Cornell University Library: How to Cite U.S. Government Documents in MLA, APA Citation Style, http://guides.library.cornell.edu/citing_us_gov_docs (free)
- ProQuest Congressional QuickStart Guide, http://proquest.libguides.com/qs_congbasic (by subscription or purchase)
- *The Complete Guide to Citing Government Information Resources: A Manual for Social Science & Business Research* by D. L. Cheney, 2002 (available in research libraries)

Two Examples

Example 1 was written at a time when cell phone use by drivers was an emerging policy problem. It illustrates an interpretive issue history written by an academic student (who was also an attorney) participating in simulated legislative lobbying. His purpose was to get the problem onto a state's legislative agenda.

Example 1

Legislative History of Banning the Use of Cell Phones while Driving

MEMORANDUM

To: North Carolina General Assembly Senator Dannelly; Representatives McAllister, Adams, B., Allen, Harrell, Hunter, Jones, Luebke, Michaux, Parmon, Tolson, and Womble.

From: AARP Steering Committee (simulated)

Date: April 7, 2008

Re: Ban on Cell Phones While Driving: A Legislative History

OVERVIEW

Driver distractions lead each year to thousands of unnecessary and pre-ventable deaths on our nation's streets and highways. One such distraction is the use of cell phones while driving. In his article analyzing legislative attempts to regulate cell phone use, Matthew Kalin cites studies that es-timate "that six-hundred thousand collisions occur each year because of cellular phone use in vehicles" and that "ten to one-thousand deaths per year" occur as a result of cell phone use in vehicles (Kalin, 262, n 21). Other researchers have compared people talking on a cell phone while driving to drunk drivers. In a 2006 study of drivers in a driving simulator, professors at the University of Utah found that "people are as impaired when they drive and talk on a cell phone as they are when they drive intoxicated at the legal blood-alcohol limit of 0.08 percent" (Strayer, Drews & Crouch, 385–90). Lives can easily be saved by banning the use of cell phones while driving.

The North Carolina legislature has made a good start in this area. Current legislation protects our children from bus drivers distracted by their cell phones (N.C.G.S. §20–140.6) and inexperienced drivers are not allowed to use a cell phone while driving (N.C.G.S. §20–137.3). Unfortunately, your bills to amend Chapter 20 of the North Carolina General Statutes to ban the use of cell phones by all drivers have not yet been passed into law.

The following review of current legislation shows that the important work of making our streets and highways safer from the dangers posed by distracted drivers has begun. Unfortunately, current legislation falls dangerously short . . . Now is the time to resume your call to protect everyone on our roads and highways from the danger posed by drivers distracted by cell phone use. North Carolina can become a leader in protecting motorists . . . by banning the use of cell phones by all drivers.

Major Legislation—North Carolina

General Assembly of North Carolina, 2005 Session

Senate Bill 1289 (Third Edition): "Cell Phone Use by Drivers Under 18 Prohibited" (G.S. 20–137.3). This Bill makes it illegal for drivers between the ages of 15 and 18 years of age to use a cell phone while driving. Specifically, this bill

- Makes the use of a cell phone by a person between the ages of 15 and 18 years of age while driving an infraction

- Provides for a fine of $25 (but does not assess court costs or result in points against the driver's license or insurance)

- Further punishes a teenage driver by not allowing the driver to advance to the next level of licensure for an additional 6 months
- Includes a ban on the use of hands-free phones, Internet gaming devices, electronic music devices, and the like.

General Assembly of North Carolina, 2007 Session

House Bill 183 (Third Edition): "Ban Cell Phone Use by School Bus Drivers" (G.S. 20–140.6). This Bill created Section 20–140.6 of the North Carolina General Statutes, making it illegal to "engage in a call on a mobile phone or use a digital media device while operating a public or private school bus" (N.C.G.S. §20–140.6). Specifically, this bill

- Makes the use of a cell phone by a bus driver a Class 2 misdemeanor
- Provides for a punishment of up to 60 days and a fine of no less than $100
- Allows for emergency exceptions

While the above protections are an important start, the AARP agrees with you that more is required. We applaud the following two bills that all of you worked so diligently on and hope you will continue your good work and see them passed into law. In fact, we encourage you to go even further in the name of safety—consider banning all cell telephone use (with the current exceptions), including hands-free phones.

Senate Bill 1399: "Ban Mobile Phone Use While Driving." This bill was re-referred to the Committee on Judiciary II (Criminal) on May 24, 2007. If passed, it would ban the use of cell phones while driving, but allow drivers to use hands-free phones while driving. It also allows for emergency exceptions and use by police, firefighters, and ambulance drivers. The use of a cell phone would be an infraction, with a penalty of a fine of $25.00. There would be no point assessment to the driver's North Carolina driver's license nor any insurance surcharge assessed as a result of a violation of this section. Also, this infraction would "not constitute negligence per se or contributory negligence by the driver in any action for the recovery of damages arising out of the operation, ownership, or maintenance of a motor vehicle."

House Bill 1104: "Ban Cell Phone Use While Driving." This bill was re-referred to the Committee on Judiciary III on May 18, 2005. If passed, it would ban the use of cell phones while driving, but allow drivers to use hands-free phones while driving. It also allows for emergency exceptions and use by police, firefighters, and ambulance drivers. The use of a cell phone while driving would be an infraction, with a penalty of a $100.00 fine and costs of court. No points would be assessed to the driver's North Carolina driver's license as a result of this infraction.

Legislation in Other Jurisdictions

According to a 2004 review of traffic safety legislation, eighteen states and the District of Columbia have passed laws regarding the use of cell phones while driving (Savage, Sundeen and Mejeur, 2004). Here is a sample of the legislation currently in effect in other states:

California: Section 23103 of the California Vehicle Code makes it illegal to operate a handheld device while driving, and the fine is $20.00 for the first offense and $50.00 for each offense thereafter (Barmby, 345).

New York: Section 1225 of the New York code bans the use of handheld cell phones while driving, and a violation of same is considered an infraction, punishable by a fine of not more than $100.00 (New York Consolidated Law Service).

New Jersey: Section 39:4–97.3 of the New Jersey Statutes makes it illegal to use a cell phone while driving unless it is a "hands-free wireless telephone." A driver in New Jersey can be cited for such a violation only if she is detained for another driving or criminal violation at the same time. A person who violates this law is to be fined "no less than $100 or more than $250" and no points are assessed to the driver's license or insurance (LexisNexis New Jersey Annotated Statutes).

In addition to state legislation, a number of towns and cities implemented their own bans on the use of cell phones while driving. Brooklyn, Ohio, was the first municipality in the U.S. to ban cellular phone use while driving, and Hilltown, Pennsylvania, also banned the use of cell phones while driving (Kalin, 244). Fort Campbell military base in Kentucky banned hand-held cellular phone use while driving (Kalin, 245). However, as you know, municipality ordinances can be overruled by a state law, "preemption," if the state legislators think it appropriate.

Again, we hope North Carolina can become a leader in providing for safer streets and highways by banning both hand-held and hands-free cell phone use while driving.

Federal Response

On July 18, 2000, Congress began hearings to discuss possible legislative solutions (Cripps, 107). The House of Representatives introduced the Driver Distraction Prevention Act of 2000, a study implemented to explore the impact of driver distractions on highway safety (Cripps, 107).

However, to date, Congress has not implemented a policy to protect drivers from the hazards posed by drivers distracted by cell phone use.

Works Cited
References are omitted owing to space limitations.

◆━• WHAT THIS EXAMPLE SHOWS. Example 1 is an issue history. It combines two organizational options, significance and trend. It shows significant current bills not acted on to illustrate a trend, a state's failure to act. The history's purpose is to call for action on current legislative proposals. The communicator is an attorney representing a (simulated) national nonprofit advocacy group advocating regulation of cell phone use by drivers. Intended readers are sponsors of proposed legislation in a state of interest. The example is part of a suite of communications in the organization's (simulated) state-by-state advocacy campaign on the topic of cell phone use by drivers.

This sample exemplifies efficient summation of legislative precedents and proposals. It shows artful interpretation. The art is to show rather than tell. Instead of assertively telling the intended legislator-readers what to do, the content motivates action by showing what is being done elsewhere.

At the sentence level, the interpretive remarks would be more concise if unnecessarily repeated words and concepts were removed. This chapter's Exercise demonstrates these revisions.

Example 2

Legislative History of the Earned Income Tax Credit

This legislative history is incorporated in a policy brief advocating reform of the Earned Income Tax Credit (EITC). Other sections of the brief are shown elsewhere in this guide (policy analysis and proposals in Example 2, Chapter 4); summary of findings in Example 1, Chapter 6).

Policy Significance and Context: The EITC and Tax Policy
As currently structured, the EITC provides a tax credit for low-income households that is based on income and family status and is fully refundable.

. . .

The original political debates in the early 1970s over the EITC reflected some differences over its primary purpose: whether to provide payroll tax relief to all low-wage workers or to increase the labor force participation of less-skilled workers who might otherwise rely on public assistance benefits to support their families, or both. Ultimately, Congress structured the tax credit to do both, but only for families with children, thus placing more emphasis on its policy role in welfare reform. In this way, the EITC fulfilled its original tenets as set forth by Congress: "an added bonus or incentive for low-income people to work," and as a way to reduce welfare dependency by "inducing individuals with families receiving federal assistance to support themselves" (U.S. Congress, Senate, 1975).

The earliest proposals for an earned income credit emerged in response to ongoing debates about a minimum income for all Americans and increasing concerns about the impact of rising payroll taxes on low-income workers . . . Traditional forms of individual income tax relief, either by reducing positive tax rates or raising personal exemptions, were of more limited assistance to those low-income workers and their families whose federal income tax liability was already zero. Policymakers began to explore whether federal income tax relief should be delivered only as an "exemption," a "deduction"—which would reduce the amount of earned income subject to tax—or as a tax credit that directly offsets tax payments or liability. Some elected officials viewed such tax assistance as part of a broader program to provide a basic social safety net and reduce or eliminate poverty—as well as a convenient administrative way to deliver cash benefits to low-income families. Others viewed this individual tax benefit more broadly as a way to offset the burdens of other taxes that all low and moderate-wage workers pay, regardless of family status, such as payroll taxes, excise taxes, state and local sales, property, and income taxes.

Under existing federal tax law in 1974, workers were not required to pay income taxes unless their incomes exceeded the amount of the minimum standard deduction plus the sum of available personal exemptions. The House Ways and Means Committee concluded in its 1975 report accompanying legislation creating the EITC: "If the problems of low-wage workers are the regressive effects of payroll taxes then the credit should be available to all low-income individuals, regardless of marital status or children" (U.S. Congress, House, 1975). The House version of the EITC covered 28 million taxpayers. In order to keep costs down, the House reduced the proposed tax credit from 10 percent to 5 percent. The one-year revenue loss was projected to be $2.9 billion, all of which would be received by workers whose incomes were below $6,000.

Whereas the House version depicted the EITC as payroll tax relief, the Senate Finance Committee's bill depicted the EITC as welfare reform. While the Senate adopted the general concept of the earned income credit, it revised it to improve "its impact on the low-income taxpayers with children" (U.S. Congress, Senate, 1975). Since many low-wage workers were from non-poor families, extending earning subsidies to all workers could be "expensive and inefficient in reaching the poor," and thus, the Senate plan restricted its subsidy to families with children and applied the subsidy to total family earnings (U.S. Congress, Senate, 1975). This change involved a revenue loss of $1.5 billion, or about one-half of the House proposal (U.S. Congress, Senate, 1975). Congress, in the end, accepted the Senate position that the "most significant objective of the EITC should be to assist in encouraging people to obtain employment, reducing the unemployment rate and reducing the welfare rolls; more importantly, most federal welfare programs apply to married couples with dependent children and it is in this area that the EITC can be most effective in reducing any tax disincentive to work" (U.S. Congress, Senate, 1975). By limiting the credit only to low-income workers with families, Congress reduced the number of potential "beneficiaries" from 28 million to 6.4 million. When the tax credit was enacted in 1975, it generated little attention. The initial credit amount was equal to only 10 percent of total income up to $4,000 (providing a maximum benefit of $400) and then it phased out at 10 percent until income reached $8,000. . . .

The EITC continued to be offered to eligible workers for the next several years and was made a permanent piece of the Internal Revenue Code (IRC) in 1978. Since that time, it has undergone significant expansions with broad bipartisan support. The credit was expanded in 1986 under President Ronald Reagan, in 1990 under President George H. W. Bush, and again in 1993 under President Bill Clinton when the size of the credit was doubled and a small credit was added for workers without children . . . EITC expansions also were used to offset the regressive effects of increases in payroll taxes and in gasoline, alcohol, and tobacco excise taxes for families with children. The 1986 Tax Reform Act explicitly cited this principle of eliminating income tax burdens for families with incomes near the poverty level as the reason for increasing the dollar amounts of standard deductions and personal exemptions. The Omnibus Budget Reconciliation Acts of 1990 and 1993 (OBRA-90 and OBRA-93) increased the credit rate, introduced a larger EITC (with a higher credit rate and more earnings eligible for the matching credit) for families with two or more children, and introduced a small EITC for childless workers. Each of these increases was phased-in over three years. Consequently, the credit rates increased every year from 1990 to 1995.

. . .

The Rise of an EITC for Single Workers

In 1993, President Clinton urged making the EITC available to very low-income workers who did not have children; opponents warned that it would be difficult to broaden the EITC to wage earners without children "without breaking the bank" . . . As part of the final legislative agreement in 1993, the EITC was extended for the first time to workers without children. In addition to offsetting a portion of these various tax increases, the establishment of the EITC for poor childless workers partially addressed a piece of unfinished business from the 1986 Tax Reform Act . . . One of those goals, often espoused by President Reagan, was to eliminate federal income taxes on workers below the poverty line so they would not be taxed deeper into poverty . . . The EITC raised the income level at which these workers would begin to owe income tax, but that level still remains below the poverty line.

After the 1994 elections, Republicans proposed several new limits on eligibility to the EITC . . . House and Senate proposals erased some of the expansion in the credit achieved by President Clinton as part of his 1993 budget plan. . . . Under the 2001 tax reforms, President Bush allowed more married couples to become eligible for the earned-income tax credit. . . . The president also proposed a permanent extension of EITC-related provisions enacted in 2001 as part of his 10-year tax cut bill.

Some reformers charge that one of the biggest challenges is the fact that the United States has become divided between a growing class of people who pay no federal income taxes and a shrinking class of people who are bearing the lion's share of the tax burden.

. . . Not coincidentally, the latest round of tax cuts follows on the Council of Economic Advisers' (CEA) Economic Report to the President, released in February 2003, which made the case that low-to-moderate income families do not shoulder a fair share of the income tax burden. The document lays the intellectual groundwork for policies that would greatly simplify the tax system, but that would arguably raise the federal tax burden on lower-income workers, while reducing that on the affluent. . . . In keeping with this, Treasury Department economists are drafting new ways to calculate the distribution of tax burdens among different income classes, and those results are expected to highlight what Bush

Administration officials view as a rising tax burden on the rich and a declining burden on the poor. . . .

As part of the President George W. Bush's Advisory Panel on Federal Tax Reform, several proposals were advanced to address the needs of low-wage workers. Robert Greenstein, executive director of the Center on Budget and Policy Priorities, focused specifically on the role of the Earned Income Tax Credit in improving tax fairness when single workers begin owing income tax several hundred dollars below the poverty line. . . .

. . .

What Role for the States?
In the absence of federal reform, states have experimented with EITC reforms. As of January 2006, 18 states and the District of Columbia have adopted Earned Income Tax Credits. Most recently, Delaware and Virginia enacted new EITCs, Illinois and Oregon changed their state EITC from non-refundable to refundable, and several states and the District of Columbia, expanded existing EITCs. In addition, three local governments—Montgomery County, Md., New York City, and San Francisco—offer local EITCs.

. . .

(The full policy brief can be found at http://law.unc.edu/documents/poverty/publications/gittermanpolicybrief.pdf.)

➤ WHAT THIS EXAMPLE SHOWS. This sample is a single law history. It exemplifies organization by trend and by chronology to characterize a pattern of legislative intent for a particular law over time. It illustrates policy analysts interpreting the records of prior reform to support a recommendation of new reform. Its message says that the recommended action fits within precedent and is possibly achievable.

Takeaway and Look Ahead

Government records research is time-consuming. For the novice, it can be overwhelming. Novice researchers need to know where to find help. Time-pressed and experienced government records researchers avoid burnout by working methodically. Chapter 6, next, shows you how to use your knowledge of the record to provide persuasive evidence in policy arguments.

For Discussion

- If you were to rank your knowledge of legislative process with a number ranging from 1 (almost no familiarity) to 10 (expert), how would you rank it today?

- Before you begin searching to explore the legislative history of a specific policy, what do you anticipate will be most challenging? After you initiate searching, what is proving to be most challenging? Where will you find help if you need it?

- The hypothetical intern in this chapter finds a Google-only search for legislative history to be unproductive. Other search tools are more productive. For a policy topic of interest to you, conduct a search of government records using Google. What are the pros and cons of using Google to search government records, in your experience?

Exercise

Clarify Sentences by Removing Repetition
First, read the original sentence taken from this chapter's Example 1 and its revision shown next, here. Then, in a document of your own, find a too-long, repetitious sentence. Revise your selected sentence by removing unnecessary repetition.

Original (Repeated phrases and ideas are italicized.)

Unfortunately, your bills to amend Chapter 20 of the North Carolina General Statutes to ban the *use of cell phones by all drivers* have not yet been passed into law. The following review of *current legislation* shows that the important work of making our streets and highways safer from dangers posed by distracted drivers has begun. *Unfortunately, current legislation* falls dangerously short in the area of *cell phone use by drivers.* (71 words)

Revision

Unfortunately, your amendments to Chapter 20 of the North Carolina General Statutes to ban the use of cell phones by all drivers are not yet law. The following review of current legislation shows that the important work of reducing risk posed by distracted drivers has begun. But it falls dangerously short. (51 words)

References

Cheney, D. (2002). *The complete guide to citing government information resources: A manual for social science and business research* (3rd ed.). Bethesda, MD: LexisNexis.

Gitterman, D. P., Gorham, L. S., & Dorrance, J. L. (2008). *Expanding the EITC for single workers and couples without children: Tax relief for all lowwage workers*. law.unc.edu/documents/poverty/publications/gittermanpolicybrief.pdf

CHAPTER 6

Position Paper: Know the Arguments

Overview

Making policy requires making arguments, often in a political context. This chapter prepares you to argue logically with evidence, to acknowledge value differences and policy alternatives, and to persuade with story telling. Writing samples illustrate policy argument supported by evidence and a story showing human impacts of a policy problem. Exercises offer practice in story telling to persuade and in tweeting to write succinctly.

* * *

A policy argument supports a claim that something should or should not be done. Such arguments have two main components: a claim and its support. The claim asserts what should or should not be done or takes a position on a debated question. Support presents the justification, elaboration, and limits regarding the claim. The argument should be intentionally constructed to convince others to accept the claim or agree with the position.

Arguments are made both implicitly and explicitly. Explicit arguments are direct. Implicit arguments are indirect, often unstated. For example, it is direct to argue that cell phone use while driving is a public safety risk. However, to argue that cell-phone using drivers should be penalized is to assume and implicitly argue that government should regulate risky behaviors. Implicit arguments are usually not intended to deceive. They are unacknowledged (sometimes unconscious) structures of thought within a position. Position takers should be critically aware of their assumptions and implicit arguments just as they are aware of their explicit arguments. Arguers should critically analyze others' positions for implicit as well as explicit arguments, too.

Why argue? In policy work, you argue to disclose what you think and what you want to accomplish. You do not argue to prove or disprove. You do not argue for or against. The popular notion of argument as a quarrel between adversaries distorts the function and significance of policy argument. So, too, does the legal notion of argument as contestation with winners and losers. In policy making, there are always more than two interested parties. In democratic process, you engage ideas, not adversaries. You argue to add your position to the debate and to the possibilities.

To illustrate, an undergraduate student government representative wants to change the culture at her university to discourage drug and alcohol abuse. As a dormitory resident advisor, she knows firsthand that campus culture encourages recreational drug use and underage as well as binge drinking. Initially, she took the position that punitive action was called for. As a member of the judicial affairs subcommittee of the student assembly, she had accomplished revisions in the university judicial system to increase sanctions against drug and alcohol use as well as penalties for violations. However, the sanctions and penalties had little impact on the character of campus life. Consequently, her position has changed. In a report that she authors for the student assembly's judicial affairs subcommittee addressed to the dean of student affairs, she now argues that judicial action is not enough. She cites evidence from dormitory life based on her resident advising experience. She claims that comprehensive action is needed to reduce dependence on drugs and alcohol for social interaction. She specifies needs to update university policy, to reorganize administration of campus life, and to design educational interventions. In her choice of proposed solutions, she has anticipated opposing arguments by other student government leaders and by some university administrators favoring either the status quo or increased sanctions and enforcement. Her purpose for arguing is to deepen the campus debate on drugs and alcohol by focusing on the central question of why campus life encourages their use.

At the same university, another undergraduate majoring in public policy studies serves as an officer of a national student association that advocates drug policy reform. In that role, she writes a policy memo to the director of a national drug control policy institute stating her association's position on recent legislation and asking the director to rethink the institute's support for recent amendments to the Higher Education Act (HEA) of 1965. (Proposals to amend typically refer to the original legislation being amended. Major acts such as the 1965 HEA are amended, often, over many years.) Those amendments barred students with drug-related convictions from receiving federal financial aid for education unless they undergo rehabilitation.

The student leader presents the association's opposition to the amendments on two grounds, fairness and feasibility. On fairness, she argues that reducing eligibility for aid to higher education hurts working-class families and discriminates against people of color. Regarding the discriminatory effects, she elaborates with empirical evidence showing that 95 percent of imprisoned drug offenders in New York State are people of color, whereas the majority of drug users are not. She interprets this evidence as showing racial bias in drug law enforcement at the state level. On feasibility, she argues that the amendments cannot be implemented because they do not call for allocation of funds to pay for rehabilitation. She anticipates rebuttals by the director of the drug control policy institute but she does not respond to them in the policy memo. Its purpose is to represent the student association's perspective on a current drug policy reform proposal.

What does policy argument do? It displays the reasoning that supports positions. It may also disclose the values that justify a position. It is important to know the differences, often subtle, between evidence-based and value-based argument. Evidence persuades through logic and rationality. Values persuade through emotion and feeling. Both evidence and appeals to values are staples of policy argument. Policy actors should know how to argue effectively and ethically using both logic and emotion. Examples 1 and 2 in this chapter illustrate.

Arguments disclose the universe of definitions of a policy problem. In practical politics, argument reveals commonalities and conflicts. These are the grounds on which a course of action can be deliberated. Commonalities among arguments can point to potential cooperation, perhaps compromise, co-sponsorship, or coalition.

Conflicts give insight into competing interests and values that must be taken into account in finding a solution.

In another illustration, a farmer has applied to local government for a permit to operate a large-scale industrial farm called a confined animal feeding operation. In the rural municipality where the farmer lives, the zoning ordinance allows such operations only as a conditional use of land zoned for agricultural uses. Conditional uses require case-by-case decisions by local officials on whether to permit or not permit the use. The decision process includes a public hearing inviting residents and others to comment on the proposed use. In the hearing, arguments including the following are made:

- Farmers have rights to use and to benefit from their property; to deny this permit is to violate the farmer's private property rights.
- Nearby homeowners have rights to use and to benefit from their property; to grant this permit is to violate the neighbors' private property rights.
- Large-scale confined animal farming pollutes the environment and creates human health risks; to grant this permit is to fail to protect natural resources and the public welfare.
- Large-scale confined animal farming is regulated and better monitored for compliance with antipollution control than unregulated small-scale farming; to grant this permit will not harm local water or community health.
- Farming is an endangered occupation; to grant this permit will enable a local family-owned farm to succeed by expanding operations and will help to preserve farming in the region.
- Farming is an endangered occupation, and industrial farming is driving smaller farmers out of business; to grant this permit is to harm the local economy characterized by diverse types of farming.

If you were a local official, how would you decide about this request? Clearly, many arguable issues and competing positions are involved. You might permit or not permit the use, basing your decision either way on a single argument. Each argument is logically supported by evidence, but potentially divisive for the community. Alternatively, you might look for commonality among the arguments and aim for a cooperative solution. You might focus on the common wishes to pre-serve private rights or to protect public health. Then you might ask the farmer applicant and the neighbors to work out a compromise. You might delay your decision until you have a revised application that takes specified risks to the community into account.

Argument has its limits in practical policy work, of course. "Arguments are made by all players all the time; as a result they have limited effec-tiveness. Although arguments are a necessary ingredient to any strat-egy, they never work by themselves" (Coplin & O'Leary, p. 107). As the local government illustration suggests, you might need to craft a political compromise along with arguing your position. Also, you must recognize political conditions that will determine your argument's ef-fectiveness. How well an argument is received has more to do with majority control in a governing body than with the quality of the argu-ment. In the local government illustration, the official who represents majority political power might have sufficient influence to force a com-promise. The minority power representative might not have enough in-fluence unless others can be persuaded to join the minority's position.

When does argument matter? Argument can make a difference at several points in the process. Arguments matter before a policy process begins, as positions are being developed. They matter at the outset of a process, as stakes are declared and agendas set. They matter again at the end of the process, when a decision is being made.

How to Argue Policy

Goal: Communicate with critical awareness of your own position and other positions, with willingness to engage other positions.
Scope: For a problem of interest, either a big picture of conditions, causes, or consequences relating to a problem or a little picture of significant particulars.
Strategy: Consider your position ethically and politically. Make a list of all the known positions on the problem. Compare your po-sition with others. Note specific commonalities, differences, and conflicts of values, assumptions, or ideas between your position and other positions.
Product: Position statement in a chosen or prescribed genre. Policy analysts inside government might choose a policy memo,

while analysts outside government might choose a news media opinion piece or editorial. Products might run to book length or they might be much shorter.

Communication objective: Reasoned argument for a position showing awareness of alternative positions and reasoning.

Task 1: Outline Your Argument

If you are authoring a position paper for a professional association or for a nonprofit organization, make sure you understand its mission and how your position relates to the mission. Be clear on that relationship. Consult before deviating from the mission.

In most cases, you can use the following outline to construct an informal argument for a policy position:

- Problem

- Issue

- Question about the issue that has at least two answers and is therefore arguable

- Claim (the arguer's assertion or answer to the question)

- Support:

  - Justification

    □ Reasons ("because," or the relevance of the assertion)

    □ Assumptions ("basis," or the values, beliefs, principles that motivate the assertion and the authority represented in the assertion)

  - Elaboration

    □ Grounds (supporting evidence for the reasons and the assumptions, which may include factual, statistical, or other evidence and appeals to emotion)

    □ Limits (constraints the arguer would place on the claim)

  - Anticipated reactions (potential responses from others holding diverse positions)

    □ Cooperative or supporting assertions

    □ Competitive or opposing assertions

    □ Altogether different assumptions

    □ Challenges to reasons or to grounds

The outline does not include rebuttal. Why? In practical policy making, rebuttal is best done during deliberation, not initially. As a policy process develops, you will have opportunities for rebuttal. Wait until all positions are disclosed. Nonetheless, your initial statement should show anticipation of reactions. Show that you are aware of positions different from your own, but don't engage them in the position paper.

Task 2: Write the Position Paper

Review the Method (Chapter 2) before you write. Be mindful of the context and communication situation for your document.

By consciously thinking about your position in relation to others (Strategy, How to Argue Policy, this chapter) and outlining the logic of your argument (Task 1, this chapter), you have already begun to plan the contents of the document. That does not mean that the document's contents should simply fill in the outline, however. Think of the outline as a skeleton. The contents are the body. Content might vary across occasions for arguing while the argument's outline stays the same.

The message is your claim or your answer to the issue question. When arguing in a policy context, be aware of your authority for making a claim. Authority in argument has two meanings, a practical, role-related meaning and a rhetorical, character-related meaning. Practically, authority means credibility and power derived from a role rather than from a credential such as specialized expertise, although that might be relevant, too. Any role carries its own kind of credibility and power, whether it's the role of holding elected or appointed office or the role of being a citizen or community member. Rhetorically, authority means persuasiveness. Authority in this sense is a function of evidence and analysis. Authority is communicated by the quality of support for claims and care for using information reliably. At their best, authoritative arguments are credible and persuasive, both practically and rhetorically.

The document must clearly show whose position it communicates. Yours? That of an organization that you represent?

You must anticipate reactions to your position. Go back to the list you made of all known positions (Strategy, How to Argue Policy, this chapter). For each position on the list, note the reaction you might accordingly expect, and then rank the reactions in order of importance to you. Remember, do not rebut in the position paper unless you are directed to do so. Keep the focus on your position.

Condense greatly for now. You will likely have later opportunity to elaborate. However, if you ignore information that readers might deem important in light of other arguments, it will cost you credibility. Possibly put detailed evidence in an appendix. Charts, tables, other graphics, or extended textual materials should normally be appended. However, the choice to append important details should rest on knowing the circumstances in which the position paper will be read and used. Writers especially should know whether all readers will see the entire document, including appendices.

Use a standard citation style for identifying sources. American Psychological Association (APA) style might be sufficient or legal citation style might be preferable.

If you are authoring a position paper that speaks for a group or organization, plan to allow adequate time for consultation. Are you the sole author, or do you have collaborators? Are you ghostwriting for someone else? Plan also to allow for review and revision, possibly multiple reviews calling for multiple revisions. Who will review drafts? Who will make revisions? Remember to check the final draft against expected standards (Checklists, Chapter 2). Check sentences for clarity (Appendix). Revise further, if needed, before releasing.

Two Examples

Example 1

In its original form, the policy brief sampled here exhibits multiple communication subgenres within a single, lengthy (55-page) document. It includes policy analysis, legislative history, critical analysis of policy discourse, and argumentation. In the following sample, only argumentation is shown. Other subgenres are shown as Example 2, Chapter 4 and Example 2, Chapter 5, this guide.

To illustrate argumentation, the brief's abstract, introduction, summary of findings, and overview of policy options are shown here. Immediately following, the argument's logic is outlined in accordance with the structure of informal argument shown in Task 1, this chapter.

Tip: The outline encompasses the entire brief, not only the excerpt shown here. You must read the entire document in reference to the outline if you want to recognize the argument's development. You have two ways of doing that. Here in Chapter 6, you can read the outline and excerpts, then flip to Chapter 4 (Example 2) and 5 (Example 2) to read other parts of the document. Refer back to the outline here in Chapter 6 as needed. Or, if that piecemeal way of reading is too distracting, go outside this guide to read the full brief. Access information is provided at the end of the sample here. Or read the scholarly article referenced at this chapter's end. As you read, refer back to the outline here in Chapter 6 to follow the argument. You must toggle between the outline and the brief or article to discern the logical structure of argument.

Expanding the EITC for Single Workers and Couples without Children (*aka* Tax Relief for Low-Wage Workers)

Daniel P. Gitterman, Lucy S. Gorham, Jessica L. Dorrance

A Policy Brief prepared for the Center on Poverty, Work and Opportunity at the University of North Carolina at Chapel Hill

January 2007

Abstract

The Earned Income Tax Credit (EITC), the nation's largest anti-poverty program, now provides tax benefits of roughly $39 billion dollars a year to over 21 million households. By supplementing the earnings of low-wage workers, the EITC "makes work pay." The EITC's popularity can be attributed to its providing both work incentives and tax relief. In 1993, Congress extended a small earned income credit to singles and childless couples; however, about 96 percent of EITC dollars still go to families with children. This discussion paper argues that, while the emphasis of the EITC on rewarding work for families with children deserves continued primacy, expansion of the EITC to childless single workers and married couples without children deserves greater attention for the following reasons:

- The disproportionate and growing income tax burden (payroll, sales, excise) faced by this group of workers;
- The growing segment of workers at the bottom of the labor market, particularly single men with low levels of education and training, who remain confined to low-wage jobs;
- The strict separation in our thinking between households with and without children requires reexamination, given the growing number of children with non-custodial parents; and,
- With a national savings rate below zero, the need to facilitate asset building for all low-wage workers, including those without children.

We recommend expanding the EITC for single workers and childless married couples with a range of policy recommendations, each targeting specific new subgroups of EITC recipients and addressing a slightly different purpose:

- Increase the EITC from 7.65 percent to 15.3 percent of earnings up to $8,080 in order to directly offset payroll taxes; and adjust the phase-in and phase-out ranges;
- Lower the age requirement for single and childless workers to qualify for the EITC from 25 to 21 to target greater workforce

participation incentives to young workers just entering the labor market and making major decisions about work;

- Encourage single low-income workers to claim the Advance (monthly) EITC and use the increase in employee payroll earnings to contribute toward health care insurance premiums; and,

- Link the EITC to asset building options such as matched savings accounts for education and training, homeownership, retirement, and entrepreneurship. In addition, remove asset limits for other public benefit programs, particularly to assist those with disabilities to enter the labor market and build assets.

Introduction

The Earned Income Tax Credit (EITC) is a refundable federal income tax credit first enacted with bipartisan political support in 1975. The EITC encourages low-income workers with children to enter and remain in the labor market by supplementing the earnings of those working for low wages, thus "making work pay." . . . In this policy brief, we explore three questions:

1. What do existing policy research and current data tell us about whether the original two goals of the EITC—payroll tax relief and encouraging employment—are being met adequately for the subgroups of childless single and married workers;

2. Are there additional rationales that would justify an expansion of the EITC for this sub-group; and,

3. What policy changes could accomplish all or some of these policy goals?

. . .

Summary of Key Findings

. . . This brief argues that, while the salient effects of the EITC on reducing child poverty and rewarding work for low-income workers with children deserve continued primacy, the potential for providing needed economic support and greater federal tax relief to childless single and married workers deserves immediate attention for the following reasons: The disproportionate tax burden faced by low-wage single workers, which has worsened since the EITC was enacted in 1975, make tax relief an even greater priority as an issue of tax fairness. . . . If any workers need a tax cut, we argue that these workers do.

A growing segment of workers at the bottom of the labor market . . . remain confined to low-wage jobs. . . . Leaving this group at the margins of the labor market undermines the strength of the workforce, communities, and families.

Policy Options for an Expansion of the EITC for Childless Workers

. . . Politically, at both the federal and state level, an expanded EITC could embody both progressive and conservative values by: (1) rewarding those who work with an earnings subsidy; (2) providing the greatest benefits to those with the greatest need; (3) offsetting the tax burden on working poor singles and childless married couples struggling to make ends meet; (4) providing incentives for people to enter the workforce who otherwise might not do so; (5) achieving these ends without increasing employer costs, without creating hiring disincentives and with minimal government bureaucracy; and (6) helping single workers and families without children, and potentially many more, to build assets for homeownership, education, and retirement when combined with other institutional supports such as matched savings programs. . . .

(See the full document including tables, charts, citations, and references at http://law.unc.edu/documents/poverty/publications/gittermanpolicybrief .pdf).

———————

►—◆ WHAT THIS EXAMPLE SHOWS. The legislator who requested this brief was considering a run for president. So, the authors used the brief as an opportunity to focus the potential candidate's attention on the small tax credit available to workers without children. Because the EITC had become a major instrument of antipoverty policy, the authors argued to extend some of its benefits. The brief illustrates authoritative evidence-based argument. It does not attempt to persuade by appealing to emotion; instead it relates (in Example 2, Chapter 4) its position to a particular set of political values. The outline presented here shows the argument's structure.

Outline of the Argument to Expand the Earned Income Tax Credit (EITC)

Problem: EITC eligibility limited to families with children.
Issue: Ineligibility of single workers and couples without children.
Question: Should EITC cover single workers and couples without children?
Claim: The EITC should be expanded to childless single workers and married couples without children.

Support

- Justification
  - Reasons
    - The disproportionate and growing income tax burden (payroll, sales, excise) faced by this group of workers;
    - The growing segment of workers at the bottom of the labor market, particularly single men with low levels of education and training, who remain confined to low-wage jobs;
    - The strict separation in our thinking between households with and without children requires reexamination, given the growing number of children with noncustodial parents;
    - With a national savings rate below zero, the need to facilitate asset building for all low-wage workers, including those without children.
  - Assumptions
    - Original policy goals of the EITC are to provide work incentives and tax relief for low-wage workers;
    - The present tax code is unfair to low-wage workers;
    - Progressive and conservative values support a safety net for people who work hard and play by the rules.
- Elaboration
  - Evidence for reasons
    - Empirical research on tax burden, job patterns, household demographics, and assets of low-wage workers.
  - Evidence for assumptions
    - Legislative history showing intent of original EITC legislation and amendments from 1975 to the present (see Example 2, Chapter 5).
    - Policy analysis of tax code (see Example 2, Chapter 4).
    - Political analysis of values (e.g., equity, efficiency, role of government) (see Example 2, Chapter 4).

- Limits
  - Political climate at the time of introducing a proposal to expand EITC;
    - If adopted, speed of implementation (might impact other anti-poverty programs);
    - Coverage (recommended solution does not cover single workers who are noncustodial parents).
- Anticipated reactions:
  - Cooperative (others might propose compatible policy changes, such as providing incentives for businesses to offer infant day care);
  - Competitive (others might argue that there are more pressing priorities, that there are better policy instruments, or for a different solution);
  - Different assumptions (replace the present tax code with a flat tax);
  - Challenges (need more empirical research and policy analysis before concluding that the tax code is unfair to low-wage workers).

Example 2

Scenario

In testimony by the Rural Coalition prepared for a 2013 Senate Judiciary Committee hearing on reform of the 1965 Voting Rights Act, the following story characterizes rural barriers to voting. For the full testimony statement, see Example 2, Chapter 9).

Larry, 38 years old, married, father of ten-year-old twin boys, and a minimum wage factory worker, drives with his family twenty-five miles from his rural community to his polling place to vote.

On the way, Larry stops for gas and pays $3.67 a gallon for regular unleaded gas, the current national gas average. After paying $25 for gas for only 6.81 gallons, the family proceeds to the polling place.

It is now 10:00 AM. Larry and his wife decide to each take a child into their respective voting booths. His wife goes into hers but before Larry can make it to his, a poll worker stops him. The poll worker tells Larry that his name is not on the voter roll. Unbeknownst to him, his name had been removed because his voter identification card was returned as undeliverable (as happened and was ruled unconstitutional in *U.S. Student Ass'n Found. et al. v. Land et al.*). Larry and his wife registered to vote last year during a door-to-door registration drive in their rural community.

Unable to vote or convince the poll worker that he is eligible to vote even though his wife was able to, Larry and his family return home, having driven fifty miles round-trip, only to have one of two votes counted for the family.

Larry and his wife sit at the kitchen table and ponder what to do. They are unaware that a Section 2 complaint can be filed with the United States Department of Justice. The United States Department of Justice's website instructs people to "contact the Voting Section at Voting.Section@usdoj.gov to make a complaint concerning a voting matter." The "Voting.Section@usdoj.gov" link is an email address. Even if they were aware, they could not send the email from their home.

The rural area Larry's family lives in does not have Internet access. Why?

National private cable providers are either refusing to provide Internet service to rural areas or planning to install it for one or two roads a year . . . Some communities have attempted to establish their own public Internet companies and have seen their efforts thwarted or complicated by cable companies working in tandem with state legislatures.

. . . Rural communities who want to build an infrastructure themselves cannot or will be hindered by the law's geographical or rate restrictions.

A few hours later, Larry and his wife try to recall a local community citizen's organization that could possibly help but one does not exist in their community. It is now 2:00 PM and both have to work in the morning at the local factory, so they scratch the idea of driving to an organization in a neighboring county. Besides, it would require more gas to drive the sixty miles to reach the organization's office.

His wife suggests they call a neighbor who lives two miles away and has dial-up Internet or travel twenty-five miles to the closest library. They decide to call the neighbor and Larry is invited over. Larry sits down at the computer and the dial-up connection fails to connect. The neighbor tells Larry to give it five or so minutes and the connection is slow.

Once online, Larry doesn't know where to go.

If Larry did, he would have to go to http://justice.gov/or use a search engine to find the site. Once there, he would have to first find on the homepage where the link to "submit a complaint" is under the "Department of Justice Action Center" section. Second, he would have to know to click on the link. Third, he would have to scroll down to find the "voting rights discrimination" link and know to click on it. Fourth, he would come to a page titled "How to File a Complaint" and either click on the "Voting Section" link at the top of the page or have to scroll down to the very bottom to find the "Voting" section. Fifth, Larry would read that he "can register a complaint [by sending] an email message to the Voting Section at Voting.Section@usdoj.gov." Even for a computer savvy person, successfully completing all these steps might prove to be daunting.

Let's say that Larry completed all the aforementioned steps. Larry may see the word "complaint" and believe he is unprepared to compose a formal email explaining why he was denied the right to vote. Furthermore, he may not have an email address because it hasn't made sense to have one since he does not have Internet access at home and therefore no computer.

So, Larry heads back home. It is now 5:00 PM.

Larry decides to call a local attorney to ask for assistance in filing a complaint. The attorney's office is thirty-five miles away and his law firm specializes in local civil and criminal law, not civil rights law. Despite this fact, the attorney invites Larry to his office but informs him that he will be charged $75.00 an hour for the consultation and drafting of the complaint.

> Larry gives up. He also decided not to vote in the local school board election that occurred ten days later.

What This Example Shows. This story represents the impacts on electoral participation of geographic isolation, inadequate public education, as well as lack of access to electricity, computers, and the Internet. Larry's story, a hypothetical composite of several actual voters' experiences, purposefully shows that policy affects real people in real ways. To represent the human impacts of a policy problem, storytelling appeals to emotion and asserts values. Larry's story asserts the value of fairness and equity.

Takeaway and Look Ahead

Persuasive argument is purposeful, credible, and accountable. This chapter tells you that policy positions supported by argumentation are more persuasive than unsupported opinion. It shows you how to argue policy positions in a political context. It demonstrates argument outlining. Using the outline shown here, you can organize your position and analyze positions other than your own.

As an experienced policy actor says, policy argument is a little like negotiation. "The process requires you to analyze your own arguments, anticipate all other arguments, and analyze them. . . . The point is to . . . understand what the interests really are. Seldom are they simple and seldom are they direct" (Helfert). Chapter 7, next, applies argument to requesting policy action.

For Discussion

- Larry's story (Example 2, this chapter) is explicit. The agriculture secretary's storyline (Illustration 1, Chapter 1) is implicit. As a reader and writer of policy argumentation, how do you feel about explicit storytelling and implicit storylines?
- Do you agree with this claim: "Definitions of policy problems usually have narrative structure. . . ." (Stone, p. 138)?

Exercises

Exercise 1: Tell a Story to Persuade
Write a story to communicate your position on a matter of concern. The matter of concern should be real. The story might be actual or hypothetical. Draw on your own or others' experience. Would you use the story to argue for new policy or policy reform?

Alternatively, write a story about a policy. The policy should be real. The story might be actual or hypothetical. Would you use the story to support or to oppose a call for policy reform?

Exercise 2: Argue Succinctly.
If you have a Twitter account, draft a hypothetical tweet (140 characters) stating your position regarding a concern of interest. Then, draft a string of tweets from varied hypothetical respondents to your position. None of these tweets will be sent out. They are only for practice in condensing your thoughts.

References

Coplin, W. D., & O'Leary, M. K. (1998). *Public policy skills* (3rd ed.). Washington, DC: Policy Studies Associates.

Helfert, D. (2014). *Policy position papers.* Instructional guide available from the author (dhelfert@verizon.net). Unpaginated.

Stone, D. (2002). *Policy paradox: The art of political decision making* (Rev. ed.). New York: W. W. Norton & Company.

CHAPTER 7

Petition, Proposal, Letter: Request Action

Overview

While legislators or administrators initiate most of it, policy can originate in other ways, too. Any citizen or organization can propose government policy or request action. This chapter shows you how to use three customary ways of communicating a request for policy: formal petitioning (Example 1), proposing (Example 2), and letter writing (Example 3). Commentary on writing samples develops awareness of metaphor in policy communication. Exercises offer practice in conceiving what you want government to do.

* * *

Action requests and policy proposals originate both inside or outside government. Nongovernmental actors might request action by petitioning. The First Amendment to the U.S. Constitution guarantees citizens' right to "petition for a redress of grievances." Over time, petitioners have come to include individual citizens as well as groups, organizations of many kinds, and corporations. Petitioning now goes beyond redressing grievances to requesting varied actions.

To illustrate petitioning, in a case of injury experienced during air bag deployment in an automobile collision, three different petitions for government action might be made.

1. A victim of chemical burns or breathing disorders attributable to air bag deployment might petition his or her congressional representatives to amend the National Traffic and Motor Vehicle Safety Act of 1966 to authorize medical training programs specific to air bags for emergency services personnel.

2. A company that has developed a new technology for increasing passenger safety without relying solely on passenger restraints such as air bags or safety belts might petition the National Highway Traffic Safety Administration to test the new technology.

3. A professional association of automotive engineers might petition the National Highway Traffic Safety Administration to reduce risk for airbag injury by amending a vehicle safety design standard to encourage seat belt use (Example 2, Chapter 10).

Another common practice for requesting action is proposing policy. Internal proposals usually convey one governmental body's request to another. Example 3, this chapter, shows a city government commission advising a mayor and city council to act. Example 2, this chapter, shows a federal agency division director requesting congressional action.

External proposals usually represent organized interest in solving a problem. The role of nongovernmental groups in North American public policy has deep historical roots. In colonial America, before the United States or its government was established, voluntary associations flourished. Associations formed to provide basic social services, to meet public needs, and to protect community interests. Voluntary fire companies, water companies, library associations, prison associations, school associations, landowner associations, and militias were so common in the America of the early 1800s that a visitor from France, Alexis de Tocqueville, observed,

> Americans of all ages, all conditions, and all dispositions constantly form associations . . . Wherever at the head of some new undertaking you see the government in France, or a man of rank in England, in the United States you will be sure to find an association (p. 106).

Such group activism provides background for the Tenth Amendment regarding limitations on central government that says "the powers not delegated to the United States by the Constitution, nor prohibited to it by the States, are reserved to the States respectively, or to the people."

Nowadays, groups that perform a public good might be granted tax-exempt status as charities or nonprofit organizations. Their function might be religious, scientific, literary, educational, promotional, protective, political, charitable, or other, in accordance with Internal Revenue Service standards for 30 categories of tax-exempt activity (Internal Revenue Service). Many, perhaps most, nonprofit organizations are not concerned with public policy. However, significant numbers of advocacy groups are active. Their methods vary according to the limitations of their tax-exempt status. Groups limited to education and outreach might communicate by legislative alerts, editorials, letters, personal visits to lawmakers, witness testimony, and more. Others, with more restricted tax benefits, might campaign for candidates running for office, lobby, and draft legislation.

Legislators and administrators often appreciate the help of advocacy groups in educating the public about needs for policy. Additionally, government staffs appreciate informed, accurate, well-argued lobbying because it helps them to brief legislators on complex or controversial issues. Legislation and regulation writers might also appreciate proposed wording, making their job of drafting legislation easier. A positive example of public good resulting from such help might be the continued strengthening of legislation in the United States on smoking as a health problem. Legislation aimed to limit smoking was passed in large part because health care advocacy groups worked with responsive legislators at all levels of government and educated the public to support directed warning labels on cigarettes, nonsmoking restaurant sections, and smoke-free public facilities. A negative example is the influence of lobbying by corporations and advocacy groups to weaken laws on occupational health and safety or on environmental protection. The milk-labeling illustration in Chapter 1 exemplifies both positive and negative lobbying.

Grassroots organizations such as neighborhood or block associations, community clubs, workplace voluntary groups, and student organizations might also use petitioning, proposing, or letter writing to accomplish their advocacy, just as nonprofit organizations might.

Why are petitioning, proposing, and letter writing important? They sustain democracy. They are democratic ways of addressing public problems by institutional means. Whether by direct democracy such as state referenda or by representative democracy such as federal legislation, self-governing society relies on public intervention in the policy making process. Remember, public policy has far-reaching effects in everyday life. Policy makers need and want in-depth information that can shed light on problems and build public support for action. Nongovernmental groups or individuals who are informed about problem causes and impacts or policy needs and consequences are excellent sources of information. While individuals can request or propose action, organized groups are likely to be more influential. They represent the power of collective interest or capacity to advise.

How to Request Action on Behalf of a Group

Goal: Policy change or government action

Scope: A group's charter, purpose, mandate, or mission will determine the concerns or issues it may address.

Strategy: Create a request for action that you conceive and frame to help a chosen organization achieve its advocacy goal.

Product: Brief written petition, policy proposal, or letter. Length varies according to purposes and situations. A short (one to three pages) document is preferred.

Communication objective: Persuade the responsible agency to act.

Task 1: Name the Need. Specify the Action and Agency.

Identify a need for policy action. If you already know the need or intervention for which will advocate, specify the desired action and the responsible agency.

If you do not know the need well, or if you have not decided on an intervention, or you are responsible for selecting from competing needs and proposed interventions, pause. Step back to focus before you proceed. Start again where necessary, whether it is to define the problem and pinpoint the issue (discovery), review the history of action or inaction (legislative history), review the arguments (analyze interests and positions), or use the Method (Chapter 2) to consider the policy context and the communication situation.

Deciding what to ask for, how to ask, and whom to ask is not simple. But it is important to get clear on all of that before communicating. Experienced advocates will tell you that much time, effort, and money is wasted in seeking unlikely action or making a proposal to the wrong recipient. The best way avoid such waste is to stop and think, as often as needed, to ask "What am I trying to do?" and "How can I do it most effectively?" That will lead to further focusing questions such as "Should I start, or start over, small (local) or big (national or international)?"

Consider the options for action; for example, if you choose government action, what do you want government to do? Government can legislate, spend, regulate, and enforce, within limits. Which type of action does your concern require? To which level of government—federal, state, local—should you direct your proposal? Which department or agency can do what you want?

Or you might consider nongovernmental options. Does the solution require government action? Are other options available? For example, a citizens group might organize a boycott or initiate a lawsuit to solve a civic problem rather than to ask for government action. Similarly, a student group might choose a community solution. For example, in response to a racist incident on campus, one student group developed a constructive plan for educating students about everyday racism in campus life. Rather than proposing it as a policy to student governance or to the school's administration, the group circulated their plan among other campus organizations and sent it to national student associations. They communicated it by word of mouth and publicized it through news media. The strategy was to ask similar student groups nationwide to draw public attention to the problem of race-based harassment on their campus and to offer as a model the original group's plan for addressing it. In this example, change in human behavior was sought through organized community education.

Task 2: Frame the Request Strategically: What, Why, How, Who, When.

Before you write a petition, proposal, or letter to initiate policy or change policy, answer the following questions. Use your answers to organize the content of your request.

- Desired outcome: What do you want to accomplish? Can you describe it as if it were already accomplished in a future you want to achieve?

- Today's situation: What's wrong in the present? Why is the action you propose needed? What causes the need?

- Relevant background: How did the problem arise? What original assumptions are no longer valid? What conditions have changed?

- Available options: What are the alternative ways of meeting the need? Advantages and disadvantages of each? Costs (money, other) of each?

- Recommended action: What is the best alternative? Can you briefly argue as to why?

- Summary: What are the results (referring to the desired future) if requested action is performed?

- Action items: Who (named) should be asked to do specifically what, when, where, and how?

Task 3: Write the Request Document

Provide only accurate, verifiable information. Anything else will destroy your or your organization's credibility and persuasiveness. Use the Method (Chapter 2) to plan and a communication that fits the intended recipients' situation. Make sure that the document's contents answer the questions listed in Task 2 ("How To," this chapter).

There is no typical form for policy proposals. If a template is prescribed by the organization you are writing for or if your intended recipient prescribes a template, use it. If not, choose an appropriate form. For any written document requesting government action, the conventions of professional communication are appropriate: identify the writer and recipient, summarize in an overview, and organize content in sub-headed sections.

The document type might be a letter, a policy memo, a full-page ad in print newspapers, animated ads in online newspapers, a public declaration dramatically delivered in historical costume, a YouTube video, or another form chosen for its effectiveness in the situation. See, for example, the websites of national nonprofit groups that sometimes express their advocacy in serious as well as funny and attention-grabbing ways. Regardless of its type, compare the finished product to expected standards (Checklists, Chapter 2).

Three Examples

These samples show petitioning, proposing, and letter writing by experts or advisers inside and outside government.

Example 1: Petition

CENTER FOR AUTO SAFETY

1825 Connecticut Avenue, NW #33a
Washington, DC 20009–5708 (202) 328–1770
www.autosafety.org
January 21, 2007
The Honorable Nicole R. Nason, Administrator
National Highway Traffic Safety Administration
400 Seventh Street, SM7
Washington, DC 20590

PETITION FOR RULEMAKING

Dear Ms. Nason:

The Center for Auto Safety (CAS) petitions the National Highway Traffic Safety Administration (NHTSA) to take action to restrict the availability of two-way communication features through in-vehicle telematic systems while a vehicle is in motion. The purpose of this petition is to make the driving environment safer by reducing the availability of devices that have been proven to be traffic hazards.

According to NHTSA spokesman Rae Tyson, "Our recommendation is that you should not talk on the phone while driving, whether it's a handheld or hands-free device." It is time for NHTSA to put the results of extensive research and its own recommendation into action.

BACKGROUND

The automotive industry has long been aware of the dangers posed by talking on a cell phone while operating a motor vehicle. Cellular telephones are an important resource for drivers who encounter emergency situations and pull off the road to make calls. However, when cell phones are used while driving, they are a significant cause of highway crashes. Many existing in-vehicle technologies . . . are being expanded to offer cellular telephone service to drivers. What was once an essentially helpful technology is becoming a source of dangerous driver distraction by the addition of personal communication features that are available to a person while driving.

In search of new profit centers, major auto companies are marketing vehicle-in-motion telematic options that degrade the safety value of the Automatic Crash Notification (ACN) originally installed in motor vehicles. For example, General Motors, which was a leader in ACN with its OnStar system, began degrading safety by including personal cell phone use as an integral part of OnStar. GM once tried expanding the scope of in-vehicle telematic systems to allow drivers to receive email, movie listings, personalized news, sport reports and weather while driving. The potential distraction is similar to permitting television monitors in the front seats of passenger vehicles, a practice that is not permitted by state law in most, if not all states.

. . .

RESEARCH STUDIES

Research has consistently shown that operating a motor vehicle while talking on a cell phone, whether hand-held or hands-free, increases the risk of an accident to three or four times the experience of attentive drivers. The general consensus of the scientific community is that there is little, if any, difference in crash rates involving hands-free versus handheld cell phones. The two-way conversation on a cellular phone, not the task of holding the phone, causes a cognitive distraction. This distraction induces "inattention blindness" inhibiting drivers' abilities to detect change in road conditions.

STATE LEGISLATION

. . .

The highest standard enacted by District of Columbia, Connecticut, New Jersey and New York prohibits the use of any handheld cellular phone but permits drivers to use hands-free wireless devices.

. . .

Many cities have encountered difficulty enforcing bans because of the high number of violations . . . The total number of cell phone calls from 1996–2001, 326 billion, shows the enormous potential exposure of cell phone use in vehicles.

. . .

EXEMPLARY VEHICLE CRASHES

No one can deny that cell phones have resulted in traffic crashes, deaths, and injuries. [Name] and [Name] were both killed when drivers talking on cell phones struck their vehicles while they were stopped at a stop light.

. . . There are hundreds of cases like [theirs] . . . NHTSA has known from the time of the first head of the agency, William Haddon, MD, that the best public health strategy is one that is passive; in this case, not permitting cell phone technology to be so readily available.

CONCLUSION

. . .

It is time for the government to intervene on this dangerous practice . . . As a first step, the Center petitions NHTSA to issue a notice of proposed rulemaking which would amend FMVVSSI02 to add a new provision reading:

Any vehicle integrated personal communication systems including cellular phones and text-messaging systems shall be inoperative when the transmission shift lever is in a forward or reverse position.

. . .

Sincerely,

Clarence M. Ditlow, Executive Director

Tyler Patterson, Vehicle Safety Intern

The full petition can be seen at http://regulations.gov
Docket ID: NHTSA-2007–28442
Document ID: NHTSA-2007–28442-0003
Date Posted: Sep 13, 2007

WHAT THIS EXAMPLE SHOWS. This external petition by a nonprofit organization of experts requests new regulation. No specific policy process is underway. That is why the petitioners ask the agency to start the process by issuing a notice of proposed rulemaking on the subject of cell phone use while driving and calling for public comment.

Example 1 illustrates in-depth presentation in compact form. It is written for reading, not speaking. One cue is sentence length. Many sentences in Example 1 would cause a speaker to run out of breath. Another cue is the extensive detail. The amount of detail is probably appropriate in this unsolicited petition.

For both petitions and proposals, the contents and length of submissions might be prescribed in a call by the receiving agency. If the agency prescribes the information and length it wants and the form it prefers, you should write as prescribed. No more and no less. Otherwise, your communication might go unconsidered.

Where to put all the details? In the main body or an appendix? To decide whether to include or append supporting information, writers need to understand the readers' situation. If the recipient prohibits appendices, do not append. If all readers will receive the whole document and (you judge that) they are willing to flip between the main text and appended information, you might append. Or, if readers are likely to receive only the parts that pertain to their role or responsibility, do not append without flagging readers' attention to look at appendices. If, after considering the circumstances of the document's reception and distribution, you decide to include everything in the main document, make sure the document's organization and expression will help readers find information quickly. Example 1 meets this expectation.

Example 2: Proposal

Scenario

Senior officers in the Surgeon General's Office have decided to make another attempt to increase Reserve Armed Force eligibility for health care. More frequent, longer lasting active deployments, increasing injury rates, and depleted state budgets for reservists' benefits justify the renewed effort. The Chief of Patient Information has been persuasive, too. So, she is now tasked to write the necessary legislative documents. Collaboration with other specialist staff will be necessary. For instance, she must gather dollar information and other numbers from the medical budget staff. When all information is in hand, she drafts a prescribed strategic planning document called a Unified Legislative and Budgeting Initiative. Before it can be submitted to her immediate supervisor, all the peer specialists in her office with whom she has consulted will review the draft. Upon submission, it will be reviewed by an eight-level chain of command beginning with her immediate supervisor, going on to the Secretary of the Army and all applicable staff experts, congressional liaison, and legal opinion to conclude, if necessary, with the Secretary of Defense. Any level of review may request changes, which she will make and then re-submit to the requesting reviewer.

FY 2011 Legislative Initiative

(Unified Legislation and Budgeting)

TITLE

Increase the Early Eligibility (EE) Period for TRICARE Benefits for Members of the Reserve Components

SHORT PROPOSAL DESCRIPTION

To initiate a Unified Legislation and Budgeting (ULB) proposal to enable Reserve Components to address the Secretary of Defense's changes to mobilization policy. Under this proposal, the effective date for the entitlement to early TRICARE benefits for members of the Reserve Components receiving alert orders to active duty would be the date of the issuance of the alert order. Current law only provides 90 days of early TRICARE benefits for members of the Reserve Components. The current 90-day authorization does not provide sufficient advanced notice to allow Reserve Component members to take advantage of this benefit. This ULB does not propose a change to TRICARE coverage for military dependents or family members.

APPROXIMATE FULL YEAR COST ($M)

The current cost of this benefit to the government is $—per service member, per year.

. . .

DISCUSSION OF REQUIREMENT AND RELATIONSHIP TO [Human Resource] HR STRATEGY

After a member is identified, screened and determined to be qualified for deployment, on average, he or she has a short time to take advantage of the Early Eligibility Period for TRICARE Benefits. If a member of the Reserve Components is identified as non-deployable due to a medical issue, the current 90-day TRICARE benefit does not provide adequate time for the medical issue to be treated. Additionally, the current benefit does not allow a service member adequate time to rehabilitate after medical treatment, thus eliminating a pool of otherwise deployable resources. As a result, the Reserve Components are overrun with service members who are unable to mobilize, leaving unit readiness diminished dramatically.

Providing an early TRICARE benefit upon the receipt of an alert order to active duty would allow for the treatment, rehabilitation, and successful mobilization for countless service members. This benefit will enable the fullest utilization of the service member's training and experience, to ensure higher levels of unit readiness. Extending this benefit will also solidify unit cohesion and allow the Reserve Components to be more responsive to wartime requirements.

This proposal would allow Reserve Component service members the maximum use of Early Eligibility for TRICARE. Increasing the eligibility period in coordination with other Reserve Component initiatives for earlier alert notification will result in higher unit readiness and higher retention of service members.

BUSINESS CASE

Reserve Component service members do not currently have adequate time to utilize this benefit to identify, treat, and rehabilitate medically disqualifying issues prior to mobilization. This has a tremendous adverse impact not only on service members and their families, but more importantly, on unit readiness and national defense.

This proposal directly supports the Army Legislative Objective to reset the Force to ensure readiness for current and future challenges with full funding to restore units to levels of readiness required to successfully execute programmed operational deployments, future contingencies, and homeland defense missions.

This proposal will enable the reserve component service members to receive preventive care and treatments necessary to become fully medically ready. . . . In addition, this will allow leadership to focus on training, mobilization activities, increase unit readiness and most importantly increase the quality of life for the service member. DOD has a high interest is seeing a fully deployable RAF force.

All seven Reserve Components have a direct stake in seeing a change in the legislation for this benefit. The Army National Guard, the Air National Guard, the Army Reserves, the Air Force Reserves, the Marine Reserves, the Coast Guard Reserves, and the Naval Reserves would be greatly impacted.

Number of Personnel Affected

	Army	Navy	Marine Corps	Air Force
Number	54,000	6,000	4,000	12,000

RESOURCE REQUIREMENT ($M)

The Early Eligibility for Medical Benefits (EE) is funded by the Defense Health Program Association Fund. Due to limited resources, the RAF does not have funding for this proposal.

. . .

Note: This proposal requires a corresponding appropriation of funding for implementation.

COST METHODOLOGY

Cost factors include 76,000 Reserve Component service members mobilized annually. The current cost of this benefit to the government is $— per service member. (This data is based on the GAO TRICARE Reserve Select report 08–104, December 2007.) Currently there are 38,700 Soldiers deployed and eligible for this benefit. The estimated funding impact to provide twelve months worth of the EE benefit is $—M.

LEGISLATIVE LANGUAGE

Current Public Law 108–136, National Defense Authorization Act for Fiscal Year 2004, section 703 states "a member of the Reserve Components who is issued a delayed-effective date active duty order or is covered by such an order for a period of active duty of more than 30 days, in support of a contingency operation, as defined in 10 U.S.C. 101(a) (13)(B)., shall be eligible, along with the member's dependents, for TRICARE, on either the date of issuance of such an order, or 90 days prior to the date the active duty prescribed in the order, whichever is later."

This proposal will change Public Law 108–136 section 703 to read ". . . the effective date of active duty for purposes of entitlement to active duty health care of members of the Reserve Components of the Armed Forces receiving alert order anticipating a call or order to active duty in support of a contingency operation, shall be the date of the issuance of the alert order for the member's unit in anticipation of the mobilization of the unit for service for a period of more than 30 days in support of a contingency operation or the date of the issuance of the order providing for the assignment or attachment of the member to a unit subject to an alert order. The member's dependents shall be eligible for TRICARE 90 days prior to the date of active duty prescribed in the order."

This proposal does not impact any other section of the law.

SECTIONAL ANALYSIS

Pros

The proposal will dramatically improve medical readiness by allowing maximum time to identify and treat medical issues that may affect unit readiness and deployability.

Service members will have an increased ability to use the TRICARE Benefit throughout the entire alert period to identify and treat medical issues and to fully rehabilitate after medical treatment. This will ensure that Reserve Component units will be at a higher state of readiness and ensure the full use of each service member's skills and training.

Cons

The cost of this proposal is over $—million over a five-year period. The RAF does not have funding for this proposal.

◆━● **WHAT THIS EXAMPLE SHOWS.** This internal proposal by a government analyst uses a prescribed template for proposing legislation. Its expression and organization fit its purpose, communication culture, and intended recipients' situation. It is generally credible in its context. The writer explains as necessary and leaves the familiar unexplained. People familiar with unified legislative and budgeting initiatives as well as soldiers' health care needs are the intended audience. Consequently, the proposal does not explain specialized terms such as TRICARE (current military health plan) or abbreviations such as FY2011 (fiscal year 2011).

The document will be discussed in meetings. Anticipating questions to be asked, the argument in Example 2 is supported by evidence of need, examination of assumptions, legislative analysis, political analysis, and cost estimation. These add to its credibility. However, the document is not ready for distribution. It is not fully traceable or accountable because it does not name the presenter and intended recipient. Perhaps, an accompanying cover sheet or other tracking sheet will name them. However, those might get lost in distribution to the levels of review. Specifying the presenter and recipient in the document is preferable.

Example 3: Letter

Scenario

The City of Tucson's Small Minority and Women-owned Business Commission [SMWBC] is made up of citizens representing for-profit businesses and nonprofit organizations. The commission advises city government. For months, tourism has been on the commission's agenda. As business owners or organization leaders living near the United States-Mexico border, commission members are aware that so-called shadow (unregulated) trade including tourism flourishes alongside sunshine (regulated) trade in the city of Tucson and Pima County. Consequences include both benefits and concerns.

The current commission chair, a bed-and-breakfast owner and operator with professional experience in international trade, acts on the mayor's request to look into issues concerning short-term private home accommodation rentals (less than 30 days) transacted by homeowners and tourists via the Internet. The commission's intent is to achieve equity in business—that is, if one business owner needs a license, then all businesses conducting activities in accordance with the city of Tucson's definition of business need licenses. To open the SMWBC's discussion, the chair voices concern that online rentals are untaxed and unregulated, in contrast to traditional tourism rentals.

After months of discussion, the commission writes an advisory letter to the mayor and city council recommending investigation. An attached memorandum details the investigation's objectives.

COMMISSION LETTER AND MEMORANDUM

City of Tucson
Small, Minority and Women Owned Business Commission (SMWBC)
July 7, 2014

Mayor and City Council
City Hall
255 W. Alameda
Tucson, AZ 85701

Dear Mayor Rothschild and Tucson City Council Members,

The Small, Minority and Women Owned Business Commission (SMWBC) has recently formed a sub-committee to explore the issues surrounding the rapid expansion of the unregulated short-term rental industry.

Our overriding concern is the protection of both vendor and consumer in rental interactions, ensuring a level playing field wherein proper business license, certificate of occupancy, insurance policies, and access to redress are standard.

The Commission asks you to consider our attached request to have City staff investigate this matter for further action. The attached memo outlines the purpose, benefits, research, regulations, and communication aspects of this proposal.

The Commission respectfully asks for your review and evaluation of this proposal.

Sincerely,

Marion K. Hook, Chair

Small, Minority, and Women Owned

Business Commission (SMWBC)

MEMORANDUM (ATTACHMENT)

To: City of Tucson Mayor Jonathan Rothschild and City Council

From: The City of Tucson Small Minority and Women-owned Business Commission

Date: July 7, 2014

SUBJECT: SHORT-TERM RENTAL (STR) PROPERTIES REGULATION

BACKGROUND/PURPOSE:

- To determine the extent to which the City of Tucson is regulating, monitoring, licensing, and collecting bed-tax revenue from all forms of short-term rentals (defined as 30 days or less). On any given day, there are hundreds of such properties for rent in Tucson. Advertising sites such as VRBO, Flipkey, Homeaway, Tripadvisor, and Airbnb had a combined total of over 1,700 listings for the Tucson region on June 12, 2014. . . .

- To create equity for Tucson short-term rentals who are currently obtaining licenses, certificates of occupancy, meeting health department requirements, safety requirements, obtaining insurance, and charging, collecting, and remitting bed tax revenue.

- To identify those short-term rentals not participating in these safety and business regulations in order to provide a safe environment for those who are on either side of this business relationship. To identify those who are not participating in the collection and remittance of bed-tax revenue.

- To develop recommendations for Mayor and Council regarding all short-term rental properties in Tucson. Recommendations to include regulation, monitoring and licensing of short-term rentals; including business license, certificates of occupancy, safety inspections, insurance coverage, and payment of bed-tax revenue.

BENEFITS

- Level the playing field for all vacation properties, including hotels, motels, bed and breakfasts, and short-term rental properties as addressed above.
- Ensure the suitability of the STR with inspection, Certificate of Occupancy, health and safety requirements and insurance to protect both the owner of the property being rented and the renter.
- Collect and remit to the City the required bed-tax revenue, Certificate of Occupancy revenue, business license revenue, event permit revenue and $2.00 surcharge per room night spent in Tucson. . . . The City could expect to collect somewhere between $500,000 and $1 million in year one with that amount increasing in future years as the City becomes more familiar with monitoring the applicable web sites and enforcing the ordinance.

RESEARCH

. . .

REGULATION PROCESS

All qualified short-term rentals:

Complete application form;

Obtain Business License;

Obtain Certificate of Occupancy;

Show Proof of Insurance;

Post Compliance Documents;

Collect and Remit Bed Taxes

. . .

FUNCTIONS OF SMWBC COMMISSION

. . .

SUGGESTED ACTION

Assign an employee or an intern to:

- Collect data and enter into a database on short-term rentals currently operating within the City of Tucson limits including, but not limited to business name, owner, address, contact information

- Distribute gathered information to City of Tucson Finance Department for distribution to appropriate regulatory bodies with City government

- Inform short-term rental business of the need for proof of business license, certificate of occupancy, knowledge of parking regulations, event licensing, alcohol service limitations, proof of appropriate insurance, business transaction tax payment, and any other information the City deems necessary

- Institute a city-wide education program via the City's web site which will inform current and future short-term rental owner of the current regulations and taxes owed

Before the commission sends its request to the council, local news reports add the topic of property rights to the discourse. Some reports argue that the proposed action will restrict home-owners' liberty to use their property as they wish.

After study, the city council unanimously agrees to investigate and calls for recommendations. The council's meeting minutes are shown next, here.

CITY COUNCIL MEETING MINUTES
Action item: Discussion to Review Unregulated Short-term Rentals (City Wide) SS/SEP09-14-179

Introductory comments were provided by Council Member Kozachik.

Information and presentation was provided by Marion Hook, Small, Minority, and Women-Owned Business Commission Chairperson, and Brent DeRaad, Visit Tucson President/Chief Executive Officer.

Discussion ensued with questions fielded and answered by Ms. Hook, Mr. DeRaad, and Martha Durkin, City Manager.

It was moved by Council Member Kozachik, duly seconded and CARRIED by a voice vote of 7 to 0, to direct staff to begin outreach with the Small, Minority, and Women-Owned Business Commission, Visit Tucson, the unregulated short-term rental industry, and Pima County, and return in 90 days with recommendations.

Citizens reading news reports about the council's vote reacted by sending email to the commission's chair. A sample follows.

"I'm withdrawing my offer of help and support for this venture. The more information I've turned up concerning city and state leads me to believe that there is no way to avoid reminding the

> city that most of the B&B's in Tucson and Arizona as a whole,
> do not pay [are exempt from] state or local taxes . . . Please let
> sleeping dogs lie or you will make a busload of enemies, includ-
> ing me. I'm sorry; in theory I agree with you but the city and
> state are so broke they would grasp at any foothold."

➼ WHAT THIS EXAMPLE SHOWS. The problematic situation in Example 3 is the "share economy" in which people use the Internet to rent their houses or spare rooms for tourist lodging or event space. What are the issues? Sharable housing is an undefined business category. Safety, liability, health, labor, and trade competition are concerns. How electronic or online commerce relates to traditional commerce is open to interpretation. Government's authority to intervene in online commerce is ambiguous. Since the 1998 Internet Tax Freedom Act (continually renewed, most recently in 2014), Congress has restricted federal and state authority to tax or to regulate electronic commerce. Municipalities lack authority to regulate it, according to the National League of Cities' 1999 resolution calling for fair treatment of local retailers in the regulation of electronic commerce. Despite unclear authority, cities such as San Francisco have initiated policy on sharable housing policy intended to nurture it.

In the Tucson example, the politics of the issue are polarized. A clue to the political discourse is the use of metaphors to frame the issues. Both the commission and the citizen use commonplace metaphors. In traditional rhetoric, commonplaces are general "common sense" claims about the nature of reality (Lanham, p. 169). In the Tucson example, proponents of regulation use sports metaphor ("ensure a level playing field") to imply an orderly, secure world. The citizen mixes grabbing and climbing metaphors ("grasp any foothold") to imply an insecure world. These expressions evoke different visions of society, one cooperative and the other struggling, potentially coercive. As rhetorical devices of persuasion, commonplace metaphors can bring people together or push them apart.

Tip: Be aware of "common sense" metaphors that occur intuitively as you write or speak. They might seem familiar and harmless to you and they might be persuasive for some readers. But for other readers they might be unfamiliar or disturbing or offensive. The point? Use metaphor deliberately, carefully, knowing that metaphor influences perception of a problem as well as perception of the writer's empathy and sensitivity (Conclusion).

The commission's initial task ended when its recommendation went to council. Having fulfilled its advisory mandate within the protocol, the commission left next steps to the mayor and council. Those steps included convening stakeholders and getting in-depth economic analysis from the city's finance department.

Tip: For controversial topics, create a communication strategy, not only single communication products. Be ready to follow up, as needed. Be aware of political protocol and local culture(s) as you plan your strategy.

Takeaway and Look Ahead

Requesting policy action is an art. Know-how includes frame awareness, political awareness, and language awareness. Artful communication includes careful and sensitive use of metaphor and story. Potentially disrespectful metaphors and stories are to be avoided. Chapter 8, next, focuses on elected officeholders as the intended audience for policy communications.

Exercises

Exercise 1: Understand What You Want
To develop your vague thinking about a need for policy into a formal request for government action, interview a policy actor about the need. Use the questions listed in Task 2 (How To, this chapter) in the interview.

Exercise 2: Find Informed Sources
If you don't know enough about an issue of concern and you want to know more, learn from policy-active nonprofit organizations. Here are some ways of getting started:

- Ask volunteer service leaders in your college or university about local nonprofits or local affiliates of national and international nonprofits active on your concern.

- Ask a librarian in your college or university library for print or online guides to nonprofit organizations active on your concern.
- Search nonprofit aggregators online. The following portals offer free searchable lists of nonprofits:
  - Urban Institute National Center for Charitable Statistics Nonprofit FAQ (overview of nonprofit organizations)
  - Guidestar (national nonprofits directory)
  - Nonprofit Yellow Pages (local nonprofits directories)
  - Independent Sector (state nonprofits directories)
- Identify congressional committees and subcommittees with jurisdiction (Chapters 5 and 9). In hearings related to topic of your concern, search the witness list for informed sources. Read witness testimony in hearing transcripts.
- Search newspaper databases for news articles that might refer to advocacy groups.

Why restrict your inquiry to nonprofit organizations? You should not necessarily limit your knowledge to one kind of source. If, for example, you are advocating for the right to use a controversial drug, you may want to enlist the support of the pharmaceutical company that manufactures the drug. While the company has a vested interest, it also might have facts and figures that could bolster or undercut your arguments.

References

Internal Revenue Service. (2014). http://irs.gov

Lanham, Richard A. (1991). *A handlist of rhetorical terms* (2nd ed.). Berkeley: University of California Press.

Tocqueville, Alexis de. (1945; 1840). *Democracy in America*, vol. 2. New York: Alfred A. Knopf.

~○

CHAPTER 8

Brief, Opinion, Resolution: Inform Policy Makers

Overview

Policy makers usually want information in short, summary form. This chapter illustrates three common types of summary document: one-page brief, opinion email, and formal resolution. Writing samples illustrate conciseness (Example 1), good/bad tone (Example 2), uses of metaphor (Example 1), and narrative organization (Example 3). A discussion topic considers politeness in policy communication. An exercise offers practice in summarizing concisely with critical awareness of language use.

* * *

Policy makers receive large amounts of unsolicited information and advice. They ignore most of it. Instead, they directly seek the information and advice they need. Issue experts and advocates can be good sources.

What kinds of information or advice do policy makers typically need? For consideration of a problem, general information might include assessments of events or conditions; arguments and critical analyses of arguments; reviews of policy options and technical analyses of the options; specialized topic reports; investigative reports; summaries of laws germane to the issue; legal counsel on interpretation of laws; and summaries of expert opinion, public opinion, and political advocacy. Beyond these general types of information, any single issue demands its own particular and detailed information.

Who provides information to policy makers? It varies by level and branch of government. In federal and state legislatures, professional staff might produce much of the needed information. The staff might consult experts, analysts, and informed issue advocates or lobbyists. Know-how, or familiarity with the policy process and understanding of the political context and interested actors, enables staff to gather information and inform legislators usefully. Staff members typically summarize their findings in briefing memos such as the one-pager shown in Example 1, this chapter. In federal and state administrations, agency professional staff follows mandated procedures for collecting stakeholder and public comments to inform regulatory decision making. Chapter 10, this guide, discusses the federal and state process of gathering formal public comment.

Municipal government differs from federal and state government in one important way, the size of staffs. Whereas large municipalities might be well staffed, smaller ones have small staffs or no staff. Consequently, local elected officials might do their own information gathering. They might utilize a range of information providers including experts (representing subject knowledge), advocacy and stakeholder groups (representing organized interests), legal counsels (representing rules and procedures), other officials and associations of elected officials (representing politics), and informed citizens (representing the opinion or experience of individuals or groups). Any of these providers might write an opinion or a briefing memo to inform an official's work.

A briefing memo or opinion or resolution should be terse and targeted. It must communicate to people who have too much to do and not enough time.

How to Inform Policy Makers in a Briefing Memo, Opinion Statement, or Resolution

Goal: Delivery of key information to target readers.

Scope: Only relevant topics in a specific, narrow context.

Strategy: Extract meaningful information from a mass of details and representation. Say what the extracted information means for the target reader's purpose.

Product: Options: One- to two-page briefing memo. Or one- to two-paragraph opinion. Or one- to two-sentence resolution. Possibly with attachments.

Communication objective: Quick reading and easy comprehension by target readers and other intended audiences.

Task 1: Develop the Information

If you are not well informed on the topic, conduct informal research:

- Attend relevant public or private meetings; take full notes; get copies of the agenda and related documents; get contact information for participants.

- Jot (in the margins of the agenda) your own notes and questions about the proceedings, and capture (as nearly verbatim as you can) the significant questions asked by others.

- Contact participants, government staff, topic experts, or knowledgeable citizens for answers to questions or referrals to other sources as soon as possible after the meeting.

If you are informed on the topic, collect information that augments your knowledge as needed or as conditions change:

- Conduct online searches for relevant research and analysis.

- Update original questions and reframe the issues as information develops.

- Pause periodically to summarize your understanding and to critically examine it. Repair gaps, correct interpretation, and recognize bias as needed.

- Continue to consult as needed to improve your understanding of the process and context.

Task 2: Write the Memo, Opinion Statement, or Resolution

Before you write, review the Method (Chapter 2). Answer its questions for your purpose and audience. Choose a genre of communication or document type accordingly.

Select and organize the communication's contents for quick comprehension and ready use by the intended audience. Do not include everything you know; this is not a test of your knowledge. Include only essentials that the information user needs and the purpose requires. You can provide more information later on other occasions.

Choose the right genre. If you are representing an organization, use its template (if it has one) for memos or policy statements. If you are free to design the communication, fit it into one or two well-designed pages. If the situation demands, you might also use a cover letter or attachments. Note: before attaching anything crucial, think about the circumstances of reception or how the document will be read and used. Attachments sometimes get detached when the document is circulated.

Review and revise drafts as needed (Checklists, Chapter 2). If you are pressed for time, revise only the overview to focus the message sharply. From the reader's perspective, the overview is most important.

Three Examples

A one-page briefing memo by an expert outside government (Example 1), emails by active citizens (Example 2), and a resolution by a nonprofit advocacy organization (Example 3) are shown.

Example 1

Scenario

An auto safety expert, formerly director of the National Highway Traffic Safety Administration (NHTSA)'s crash investigation program, perceives need for better information to improve highway safety analysis. In his opinion, police reporting of accident investigation routinely lacks crash and injury severity information that experts need to analyze crashes. While in office at NHTSA, he initiates an effort to reform the reporting procedure. His objective is to improve detail and specificity in the standard report form by utilizing updated communication technologies. His idea goes nowhere. Resistance to changing longstanding reporting practice prevails. After his retirement from government service, his idea is endorsed by two organizations, the Center for Auto Safety and Advocates for Better Highway Safety. Then, to get policy makers' and regulators' attention, he writes brief, pointed communications as an outside expert. Here, a one-pager is shown.

Bring Police Crash Investigation and Reporting into the 21st Century

We in the road safety community are effectively driving blind. Why? Because technological advances in police capabilities and practices are not utilized in police crash investigation and reporting. Information that safety analysts and others need in order to improve road safety is typically not collected. However, it could be collected by the updated approach proposed here.

Background

Police Accident Reports (PARs) provide basic data on the drivers, vehicles, crash location, weather and lighting conditions, personal injury, property damage, and more in brief, often handwritten documents without photographs. Key variables for safety analysis such as the severity of crashes and injuries are not included.

Opportunity for Change

The National Highway Traffic Safety Administration (NHTSA) is struggling with how to improve its national crash data systems. These systems rely on PARs to provide data (such as the Fatality Analysis Reporting System) and as a basis for case selection for detailed investigation (the National Automotive Sampling System). Police investigations are critical because they have access to fresh information on a crash and the authority to collect such data. NHTSA's systems are stymied by the lack of detail about crash and injury severity in a PAR.

Updated Approach

The handwritten, insufficiently detailed PAR is antiquated. Six current technologies could dramatically improve PAR quality and detail:

- Hand-held computer software could support electronic data input and guide investigating officers as they collect data and report on crashes.

- Digital photography can provide visual evidence of vehicle damage and other crash conditions. Artificial intelligence can make a reasonable (and critical) estimate of crash severity from visual evidence.

- On-board crash recorder data on pre-crash speed, braking, and belt use, could be easily downloadable by investigating officers with a computer or cell phone–based app.

- Satellite images of a crash scene can be downloaded from the Internet and, with computer drawing tools, would enhance scene diagram detail and quality.

- Internet communications can support timely transmission of electronic PARs to state databases, prosecutors, insurers, and NASS investigators.

- Artificial intelligence could be developed to make estimates of the collision deformation classification (and hence crash severity) as well as injury severity (see TraumaHawk).

Benefits include better law enforcement; insurance settlements; assessment of highway safety challenges, and evaluation of safety programs, vehicle safety improvements, and driver behavior. Costs of new equipment and training could be covered by §405 state Highway Safety Program grants.

The National Safety Council recently published a paper making similar, but more limited recommendations.

© Carl E. Nash, PhD: Washington, DC, May 2017. By permission.

➤ **WHAT THIS EXAMPLE SHOWS.** Brevity in this one-pager is enhanced by sectioned content, subheadings to mark topic changes, and economical sentences. Each sentence emphasizes one idea, one actor, and one action (Appendix).

In addition, an overview efficiently summarizes the document's message without details. Readers have the choice of reading only the overview or reading further if they want details. (The sample's author, an experienced governmental communicator, knows that recipients might read only the overview.) Features of the overview's efficiency include:

- short, declarative opening sentence using a metaphor ("driving blind");

- question-and-answer format ("Why? Because . . .")

- sentence fragments in conversational style ("Because . . .")

A caution about the metaphor "driving blind." This prominently-placed metaphor forcefully expresses the writer's perception. It might get the reader's attention. However, its use should be carefully considered. "Driving blind" is commonplace expression, but it is not neutral. It might convey insensitivity toward people with sight disabilities. And, potentially, as driverless cars become reality, the expression might become meaningless. *Tip*: Metaphor can subtly support or undercut a message. Writers should be alert to the pitfalls of using common metaphors in public sector communication. For another cautionary instance, see Example 3, Chapter 7.

Writers also need to be alert to using common words that have multiple meanings. The writer of Example 1 uses *critical* in two senses, urgently important ("investigations are critical") and analytical ("reasonable [and critical] estimate"). If this multiplicity of meanings for a key term is intentional, the deliberate ambiguity should be explained in context.

Example 2

Tone matters in opinion statements. In the following email messages to an elected official in county government, tone affected the messages' reception and response.

Good tone. These three opinion statements got the policy maker's careful attention and received a substantive reply.

A. You currently face a difficult decision regarding the proposed merger of [Town and County] Schools. I am writing to suggest a public referendum on this matter given the significant impact that the results of your decision will have on your constituency. Thanks for taking time to consider this request.

B. The merger discussion is heating up quickly, and I'm hoping the real issue of the disparate funding for the two systems doesn't get lost in the commotion. The push for a referendum, called for by so many [Town] parents, seems a veiled attempt to simply stifle discussion, allowing the real issue to again get swept under the rug, still unfixed.

C. Here are a few questions I'd love to have answered. I know you're busy and probably receiving hundreds (??!!) of emails daily on this issue. I hope you can fit me in.

  1. Do you see a funding imbalance between the two systems? . . . We need a solution. Thank you for considering my questions.

Bad tone. In contrast, these three opinion statements (like many similar ones generated by a letter-writing campaign) got little attention and received no reply.

A. I understand that the [County] Board of Commissioners is evaluating a merger of the [Town and County] School Systems. I would like to communicate that:

  • I, along with most of my local colleagues and neighbors, are vehemently OPPOSED to a merger.

- I request that a public REFERENDUM be held on this issue ASAP.

- Unless proper procedure is followed throughout, a proposed merger will be challenged in the [State] and Federal courts to the extent necessary.

- The voting records of the entire board will be well remembered and publicized in time for the next ELECTION.

B. I am greatly disappointed in your decision Wednesday night to short circuit democracy in our county. None of you ran last November with a position on school merger. You have suddenly sprung it on the citizens of the county. Since you would not face voters on the issue, you should allow a referendum on the issue in the county. Otherwise, you should delay the issue until an election year, and run on your beliefs. The idea that you can have a "stealth" merger of school systems and avoid the will of the citizens of the county, as some of you seem to believe, is not in keeping with the traditions of transparency and progressive politics in our county. I voted for you all last November. But I did not vote for school merger. Now I feel that your election was as much a sham. I would like a chance to vote on school merger or to vote again on your positions on the county commission.

C. I am very concerned about an article in the Herald which indicates that the schools in [County and Town] may merge. I don't understand what the advantage of such a move would be. If there is an advantage to the move please let me know what it is. If there is no advantage to the move, please let me know by ignoring this message.

WHAT THESE EXAMPLES SHOW. These emails teach communicators to make careful choices. A public policy communicator must make many competing choices: purpose, contents, presentation style and tone, medium of delivery, and concern for immediate reception and use as well as for the permanent record. The choices are important because the consequences are significant.

Communication is more than an information exchange; it is also a social interaction. Empathy or writers' awareness of readers' circumstances affects a communication's reception. Tone or the perceived attitude of a text has a big effect. (A wise communicator once said, "People might remember what you write or say to them.

They certainly remember how you make them feel.") Recalling that policy makers receive lots of unsolicited communications and have too little time to absorb needed information, you should be aware that tone explains why some communications are ignored and others are considered. Emails that are expressly hostile or that seem closed-minded are not likely to be read, to receive a response, or to be useful to the process.

Example 3

In this example a nonprofit organization empowers its members to participate in policy making. The development of policy starts with an individual member who cares deeply about an issue. The scenario shows the process he follows to achieve consensus and craft an organizational policy statement at state and national levels.

Scenario

After years of working in finance and international banking in Tokyo and New York, an economist returned to farming and political activism in his home state, Wisconsin. With his wife and family, he now sells cattle as a cash crop and vegetables as value-added farm products for local markets. Distressed by the continued worsening of farm economics in which farm wealth is transferred to profits for manufacturers or subsidies for U.S. consumers, he tries in various ways to invigorate economic support of family farming by the Wisconsin Farmers Union (WFU). He works to strengthen advocacy by the National Farmers Union (NFU) for structural changes to revitalize agriculture. As a WFU director and NFU policy committee member, he regularly draws on his experience in banking, finance, and farming to draft policy positions. He writes issue analyses for farming publications and he proposes resolutions to the state WFU and the NFU. He shepherds the resolutions through the NFU's hierarchical, deliberative policy making process.

Here's how the NFU policy process works: Members submit draft policy proposals to the NFU resolutions committee, preferably through a state chapter president or delegate, in February prior to the annual national convention in March. The proposals may have been already adopted by a state chapter of the NFU or they may originate at the national level. Alternatively, a member may submit a proposal at the annual national convention by going before the resolutions committee with draft copies and persuading the committee to bring the proposal to the convention floor. Or, a member may bring a proposal to the floor directly (best if presented by an official delegate) with enough copies to distribute to all delegates in attendance.

On the floor at the appropriate time that delegates are reviewing and voting on outstanding policy, amendments, and addenda according to procedure stated in the NFU policy manual, the proposer is given two or five minutes to explain and advocate the policy proposal. Delegates may respond, question, or criticize the proposal. The proposer is then given two minutes to respond. Under Robert's rules of order, the proposal can then be motioned, seconded, and openly discussed. As the proposer in this example remarks from experience at state and national conventions, contentious discussion might carry on for an hour or more until a vote is called.

In 2014, this proposer offered five resolutions. The NFU adopted one, a resolution advocating reduction of profit taking by agricultural manufacturers. That resolution is shown here in proposed and adopted forms.

RESOLUTION. PROPOSED WISCONSIN FARMERS UNION POLICY

"Excessive Profit-Taking by Manufacturers of Farm Inputs"

- Whereas the manufacturers of fertilizer and seed in the case of grain farming have benefitted excessively from historically cheap cost of production and high net sales prices;
- Whereas these manufacturers have generated over the past five years gross margin ratios in excess of 40% and returns on equity exceeding 20% while farmers earn on average historically equity returns of 2 to 6 percent;
- Whereas major farm equipment makers over the past five years have shown returns on equity between 20 and 30 percent;
- Whereas our farmer cooperatives have roughly demonstrated returns on equity around 10 percent;
- Whereas we as farmers are increasingly transferring wealth off our farms with time-risk factors far greater than manufacturers

of farm inputs and we are effectively subsidizing and padding the bottom lines of these manufacturers and agri-business;

- Whereas the growing phenomenon of concentration of wealth and income in the US in the hands of a few to the detriment of the majority, particularly the middle and lower classes, is demonstratively witnessed in increasing profitability of farm input manufacturers;

- Whereas if profits are not raised for farmers, there will be increasingly a concentration of farm production in fewer producers and force more small and mid-size traditional farmers from the industry.

The Wisconsin Farmers Union hereby calls for pressure and influence to be placed on manufacturers of farm inputs by our members and our member-controlled cooperatives to reduce manufacturers' level of profitability at the expense of farmers with their diminishing returns and to advocate that our congressional representatives reduce or eliminate tax benefits and credits afforded by Congress to companies earning enormous return ratios.

ADOPTED NATIONAL FARMERS UNION POLICY

"Profit-taking by Manufacturers of Farm Inputs"
We call for all farmers and member-driven and -controlled cooperatives to place pressure and influence on manufacturers of farm inputs, whose level of profitability comes at the expense of farmers. (https://nfu.org/2017-policy/#Article3.E)

━━━━━━━━━

►━• WHAT THIS EXAMPLE SHOWS. In governmental communication, resolutions are substantive as opposed to procedural. Resolutions express a body's approval or disapproval of something that it cannot vote on because it lacks jurisdiction or because the matter is being handled by another body. Resolutions identify applicable principles, but they do not address methods and means of enforcement. Proposing a resolution is an appropriate way to articulate values, whether or not they are actionable.

As political expression, the WFU proposed resolution strategically uses symbolic representation in the form of naming, narrative or causal story, and numbers. The writer names the issue "excessive profit-taking" to connote extremity and imbalance. That issue contributes to a problem that policy might help to solve, the decline of family farming. In the causal story, excessively profitable manufacturers and subsidized consumers are the bad guys; farmers are the good guys. Numbers or percentages of profitability are the details that tell readers how the bad guys' profits depress the good guys' profits. In this story, traditional family farms are the victims, and manufacturers along with subsidized consumers are the villains. Naming and narrative are deliberately used for their emotional power in this example. They show a skillful interpreter of agricultural economic conditions defining a problem in compelling terms. The terms imply threat to values of fairness and balance. In summary, the WFU-proposed resolution uses multiple devices to express a perceived need for action.

Notably, the NFU-adopted resolution omits these devices and shrinks the scope of recommended action. Emerging from the national organization's policy process, the adopted resolution is terse. In few words, the NFU states its consensus on the issue. The resolution's scope is wide, however. By adopting and publishing the resolution in its policy manual, the NFU authorizes members nationally to pressure manufacturers of farming supplies. As added value for political communication purposes, the policy statement's simplicity and brevity make it useful for referral when NFU members lobby elected representatives. In face-to-face meetings with legislators and their staff, NFU members can fill in the picture with details of their economic situation as farmers.

Takeaway and Look Ahead

Opinion and information are vital to policy making. Useful information in a purpose-oriented, targeted communication has the best chance of getting through. A one-pager is the written equivalent of a one-minute "elevator speech" or oral summary of testimony. An email opinion is the equivalent of a voicemail message. A resolution is the equivalent of a public announcement. The tone of such communications should be professional and polite. Politeness is valued in the culture of public policy making. Concision or limitation to necessary words is also valued.

In Chapter 9, next, you'll learn about another communication type, testifying as a witness in public hearings. The interaction is face to face under time constraints. In that context, politeness and concision matter greatly.

For Discussion

What is gained or lost by polite expression in policy making? Who decides what is polite and what is not?

Do expectations of politeness differ for written and spoken communication?

Exercise

State Your Position Explicitly and Respectfully

Draft a one-pager, or a one-paragraph email, or a one-two sentence summary to state your position on a concern. As you draft, notice your language choices and decisions. Is your position stated explicitly? Where?

Is each word necessary? Does each detail support the point? Are figurative devices (metaphor, synecdoche, narrative) used? Will any of the devices be misinterpreted?

How might the recipient feel when reading your communication? How will they perceive you, the writer?

~⊃

CHAPTER 9

Testimony: Witness in a Public Hearing

Overview

Public hearings offer a rare opportunity for direct interaction between elected officials and expert witnesses. Witness testimony can be powerful communication in a policy process. This chapter describes hearing preparation, testimony writing, oral delivery, and responses to questions. Samples illustrate strategic word choices (Example 1) and story-telling (Example 2) to support a testimony message. An exercise invites you to observe the communication dynamics of a congressional committee hearing.

* * *

In the U.S. federal government, "sunshine" or public access laws mandate open hearings for all legislative functions—making law, appropriating funds, overseeing government operations, investigating abuse or wrongdoing, and approving nominations or appointments to office. Hearings are held in executive and legislative branches of federal government. In state and local governments, public deliberation is mandated, but public hearings are not commonly held except for specific actions that require public comment. Adoption of a local ordinance requires a hearing, for example.

In government bodies organized by a political party structure such as the U.S. Congress, the majority party (the party in power) chairs committees and thus sets the agenda for committee work, including public hearings. Committee chairs (with their staffs) decide whether to hold a hearing on a topic within their jurisdiction, what the purpose of a hearing will be, and who will be on the witness list. Topics and purposes of hearings reflect the committee's jurisdiction and the chair's political agenda. The agenda might or might not reflect cooperation between the majority and minority interests of members on the committee.

Several committees might hold hearings on different aspects of the same topic, especially if the topic concerns a hot issue that crosses jurisdictions. Hot issues are those that are currently in the news, controversial, or especially significant in some way. Most hearings are not about hot issues, however. Most hearings are workaday sessions to oversee government operations, to decide on appropriations of funds, to reauthorize programs, and so forth. They do the routine work of governance.

Public affairs television usually does not broadcast these routine hearings. Selected daily hearings are summarized on the government page of newspapers and some advocacy group websites. Some congressional committee websites broadcast hearings in progress.

In the executive branch, departments or agencies hold public hearings on issues within their regulatory responsibility. Some are held in the field, in geographic areas or political districts directly affected. Executive branch hearings vary in format from informal public meetings to formal deliberative sessions.

In principle, anyone might be invited to testify who can provide information that lawmakers or administrators seek. In reality, witnesses testify at the federal level only by request of the committee. At state and local levels, the witness list is more open. There, you may be invited, or you may ask, to testify. If you wish to testify, you contact the staff of the committee or the agency holding the hearing.

In the communication situation of a typical hearing, witnesses testify as spokespersons for an organization or a government agency. Occasionally, individual citizens testify on their own or their community's behalf. Witnesses must relate their special concerns to a policy, their agendas to other agendas, and their testimony to the purpose of the hearing.

Policy makers and witnesses interact face to face, and exchanges might be polite or confrontational. Questioning might be focused or loose. Questioning is always political, and sometimes it is bluntly partisan. The atmosphere might be orderly or hectic. The time limits are always tight—typically one to five minutes for each witness to present testimony and five minutes for each member to question all the witnesses. There might be multiple rounds of questioning. Hearings can last for hours or days if the committee or the witness list is large.

Legislative hearings are characteristically more free-form than legal hearings. Unlike law court proceedings, in legislative hearings there are no prescribed rules for disclosing evidence or for objecting to questions. Exceptions are legislative hearings to investigate governmental fraud, abuse, or wrongdoing in which witnesses might testify under oath. Even then, questioning is not constrained by rules. Consequently, witnesses in legislative hearings must prepare well for anticipated and unanticipated developments in the question-and-answer session that follows testimony statements (Smith).

Everything communicated in a hearing goes into a transcript (via a legislative stenographer). This transcript is the official public record of the hearing. Unofficially, the hearing might be broadcast and reported by news media followed by commentary in all media. These influential accounts shape public discourse and the perception of problems; however, they are not authoritative. They would not be included in a legislative history, for example. For the authoritative and official record of a hearing, a stenographer records the statements, questions, and answers verbatim, exactly as they are given. In current legislative reporting practice, the verbatim transcript cannot be edited except to correct factual errors. The transcript is later (sometimes months later) printed and published by the superintendent of government documents through the government printing office. This is the legal record of the hearing.

Published hearing records are important for democratic self-governance because they give continuing public access over time to the accurate and full information produced by a hearing. That information is useful for many purposes. Journalists, law clerks, academic researchers in many fields, legislative staff, lobbyists, advocates, and active citizens use hearing transcripts as sources. Published hearings are primary sources for legislative history research, for example. They are also major sources for determining a law's original intent when the law is being adjudicated.

Why do open hearings matter? For witnesses, they offer a rare opportunity to bring concerns to the table, to talk directly with policy makers, and to make personal or professional knowledge useful for solving public problems. For policy makers, hearings offer a rare opportunity to talk directly to knowledgeable witnesses. In contrast, most information policy makers receive is filtered through staff or advisors or lobbyists.

How to Deliver Oral Testimony Based on a Written Statement

Goal: To speak authoritatively and to answer questions responsively in public deliberation.

Scope: The purpose of the hearing determines the testimony topics and questions to be anticipated.

Strategy: Prepare, prepare, prepare. Be ready for questioning, the most important part of the hearing.

Products: Two expected products are a short oral summary (either a list of talking points or a one-page overview to be read aloud) and a full written statement to be included in the record of the hearing.

Communication objectives: Bring a particular viewpoint to bear on the hearing's topic and purpose. By effective testimony and credible answers to questions, gain consideration of your viewpoint and information.

Preparation to Testify

Obviously, witnesses must know their subject and their message. Equally important, witnesses must understand the purpose(s) of the hearing and their own role and purpose(s) for testifying. Effective witnessing is achieved by presenting concisely and by responding credibly to questions. Responding to questions is most important. If you are on the witness list, you are acknowledged as having something relevant to say. You do not need to impress people by showing how much you know about the topic. Instead, focus strongly on your purpose and your message in relation to the hearing's purpose. That approach leaves you free to respond to unexpected as well as expected developments in the interaction.

Know the context. To what policy process does the hearing relate? To what political agenda? Who's holding the hearing? What is the stated purpose of the hearing? What is the political purpose? Will witnesses be placed under oath? Who else is on the witness list? What are their messages likely to be?

Know your message. Distill your message into one to two sentences that you can remember and can say easily. How does your message relate to the purpose of the hearing? How does it relate to other witnesses' messages? Anticipate committee members' responses and questions. What might they ask you?

Know your role. Are you speaking for an organization? For yourself? Why are you testifying? What do the organizers of the hearing hope your testimony will accomplish?

Know the communication situation. Will the press attend the hearing? Are you available for interviews after the hearing? Will the hearing be televised? How is the hearing room arranged? Do the arrangements allow you to use the charts, posters, or slides? Are those visual aids a good idea if the room lights cannot be dimmed because of televising the hearing? What is the location for the hearing? If you are using charts, posters, or slides, how will you transport them? Who will set them up in the hearing room?

Rehearse your delivery. Will you read your statement or speak it? Generally, speaking is preferred. Be ready to do either, however. Some committee chairs want witnesses to read their statement so that members can follow along in the document as you read. Rehearse before the hearing by reading the full statement aloud and by speaking from an outline. You'll discover which way is easier for you and which you need to practice more.

Task 1: Write the Testimony

Use the Method (Chapter 2) to plan testimony in both oral and written forms. Some witnesses prefer to outline the oral summary first and then to write the full statement from that outline. Others prefer the opposite way. They write the full statement first; then they outline an oral summary based on the written statement.

If you choose to start with the oral summary, write it out. Even if it is simply a list of talking points on an index card, write it. As you testify, the list will provide confidence and control. Recall that everything said in a governmental public hearing is recorded and that the record is made publicly available. Do not plan to wing it or to summarize extemporaneously. If you do that, you risk exceeding time limits; committee chairs do not like that. Worse, you might forget important information, or say more or less than you intend to have on the public record, or open yourself to questions that you are not prepared to answer. If you are free to organize your testimony, you might use the following template. Use it in outline form for the oral summary, and expand it appropriately for the full written statement. Put extensive support in appendices, not in the main statement. (Both the oral and the written versions will be included in the transcript of the hearing.) Here is the template:

- Title page or header to identify the organization and the witness, the agency holding the hearing, the topic, the date, and the location of the hearing;

- Greeting to thank the organizers for the opportunity to testify and to state why the topic is important to the witness;

- Message to state the main information the testimony provides;

- Support (evidence, grounds) for the message;

- Relevance of the message to the hearing's purpose;

- Optional: discussion or background to add perspective on the message (only if relevant or if specifically requested by conveners of the hearing); and

- Closing to conclude the testimony and invite questions.

Task 2: Write the Full Statement

The written statement might use the same organization as the oral summary. The written statement may be longer, include more details, and be accompanied by appendices. It can be any length, but it should be no longer than necessary. Even if the written statement is lengthy, it must be organized and concise. Good organization enables you to condense on demand. If, for example, you have planned to read the full statement but you are asked by the committee chair to limit your remarks, you are prepared to condense on the spot. To condense, state your message, state its relevance to the hearing's purpose, and conclude by saying that you will be glad to answer questions.

Task 3: Present the Testimony

The following tips are important.

- Summarize. During oral delivery, whether reading a document aloud or speaking from an outline, state only the essentials. Save the details for the question-and-answer period.

- State the message early and emphatically. Whether reading a text or speaking from an outline, state the message up front.

- Stay within time limits. Usually, the chair of a hearing will tell you the time limits. If not, assume that you have two to five minutes for a summary. Do not go over the limit. If you go over, you will reduce the time given to other witnesses and to question-and-answer.

- Listen. Pay attention to the opening statements by the committee chair and the committee members. Opening statements cue the questions that you might be asked. Or they might include content to which you want to respond later, when it is your turn to speak. Listen also to other testimonies. Committee members might ask you to comment on other witnesses' remarks.

Tip: When you have presented your testimony statement, you are not finished. Shift your attention to questioning. The question-and-answer time is the most important part of a hearing. Committee members and witnesses alike agree on this. For committee members, it is a chance to question knowledgeable people directly. Members usually ask prepared questions to get important concerns, as well as witnesses' responses to the concerns, on the record. For witnesses, the question-and-answer time is a chance to connect their message to varied agendas represented in the questions or to emphasize the usefulness of their knowledge to the committee. Stay alert and follow these guidelines:

- Listen to the questions asked of other witnesses. Do not daydream or otherwise lose focus while others are being questioned.

- Make sure you correctly hear each question put to you. If you are not sure you heard the question correctly, ask to have it repeated.

- Listen closely to the question. Answer the question that is asked, not some other question that you half heard or that you prefer.

- If the question is unclear (or, possibly, off-base) and you don't wish to have it repeated or to embarrass the questioner, preface your answer with "As I understand the question . . . ." This polite tactic achieves several objectives: it shows that you are responsive and it invites the questioner to rephrase thus giving you another opportunity to respond.

- When you have answered a question, stop. Do not elaborate. Wait for a follow-up question. Postpone elaboration or qualification on your original answer until a follow-up question invites you to provide them.

- Do not lie or invent information. If you hear yourself fabricating an answer (perhaps out of nervousness), stop. Politely ask to have your answer removed from the record and begin again.
- Handle these situations especially carefully:
  - You are asked for your personal opinion. When you testify as spokesperson for an organization, be careful to present the organization's viewpoint. Avoid giving a personal opinion unless specifically requested, and then only if you appropriately can do so. If you do, be careful to distinguish your own view from that of the organization.
  - You don't know the answer. Depending on the dynamics at the moment (neutral or friendly or confrontational) and considering the effect on your credibility of not answering a question, you might choose among these options: simply say you do not know; say you are not prepared to answer but can provide the answer later; ask whether you might restate the question in a different way that you can better answer, or defer to another witness who can better answer the question.
  - Your credentials are challenged or your credibility is attacked. Do not get angry. Politely state your or your organization's qualifications to speak on the topic of the hearing. Restate why the hearing topic is important to you or your organization. Maintain your role in the hearing as a source of information and perspective not offered by others. Maintain your composure.

Two Examples

Example 1 on military healthcare benefits was written by the professional in federal government shown previously (Example 1, Chapter 3; Example 2, Chapter 7). Example 2 was written by a law student intern for a nonprofit organization. Scenarios remind you of the context for Example 1 and introduce the context for Example 2.

Example 1

Scenario

The Office of the Chief Surgeon, Reserve Armed Forces, is asked by interested congressional offices to justify the request for increased health-care benefits for Reserve Component Soldiers. The House Armed Services Committee asks for a witness to testify in an upcoming hearing, specifically to justify increased dental-care benefits. Senior officers are unavailable to write the testimony. The chief of patient information is asked to draft a statement making the case for more dental care. A senior officer will orally deliver the testimony as witness. Delegation of writing or "ghost-writing" is characteristic in her workplace as in others. The work of many professionals may be present, unidentified, in a document that carries only the organization's name and perhaps the name of the head administrator.

This action officer has not previously written congressional testimony. She is uncertain about the genre. Also, she does not know the committee's political agenda and related purpose for this hearing. She has little experience in writing for congressional audiences. She has not attended a hearing. There are no guidelines for writing congressional testimony and there is no template for a witness statement in the Army manual of procedure or style.

As an astute professional communicator, however, she knows that context, genre, purpose, and audience are as important as message. So, despite a hectic schedule, she makes the time to prepare for writing. She consults textbooks on policy writing and government writing. She searches the Internet for samples of testimony by government witnesses. Reading actual samples gives her a feel for the expected form. Asking experienced peers about the committee holding the hearing gives her a sense of the context.

She drafts a statement and circulates it in her office for specialist review of content. She also sends it to a friend in another office, an experienced staff member for a senator who serves on relevant committees. The friend provides informal contextual review. Once formal review by staff is completed, the document comes back to the action officer. She makes all changes, and then she gives the document to the senior officer who will be the witness. He reviews and requests changes, which she makes. She briefs the witness on the testimony's topic. Before the committee hearing date, a mock hearing will be held involving key participants from all agencies who reviewed the statement.

UNCLASSIFIED

Statement by Colonel Michael Flynn

Chief Surgeon of the Reserve Armed Forces of America

Before the House Armed Services Committee

Subcommittee on Oversight and Investigation

Second Session, 110th Congress

on

Dental Readiness in the Reserve Armed Forces of America

May 17, 2008

Chairman Smith, Ranking Member Clay, as the Chief Surgeon of the Reserve Armed Forces of America, I am here today to answer your concerns about the dental readiness of the Soldiers in the Reserve Armed Forces of America.

The interest of the subcommittee on this issue is well placed. Dental readiness of our Citizen-Soldiers is a critical element in their capability to meet Department of Defense requirements for deployment.

Current Situation

The transition from a Strategic Reserve to an Operational Force has placed tremendous strain on the Reserve Armed Forces of America. Historically, as a strategic reserve, Soldiers and leaders of the Reserve Armed Forces addressed dental readiness issues at the mobilization station. The implementation of the Department of Defense's twelve month mobilization policy in February 2007 forced units to address dental readiness at home station in order to maximize collective training at the mobilization station.

The Reserve Armed Forces Medical Team, in conjunction with our Armed Forces Dental Command partners, has successfully managed this transition to an Operational Force. Since the beginning of the fiscal year, our units have prepared seven Brigade Combat Units (BCUs) for deployment, with each unit sending their units to the mobilization station over 90% dentally ready. These incredible readiness rates are a tremendous improvement over their previous mobilizations in 2003, when the average dental readiness rate was 13%. This significant decrease in the number of training days lost to dental treatment at mobilization station has enabled commanders to focus on collective training and maximize boots-on-ground time in theater.

Due to the low level of baseline dental readiness in the Reserve Armed Forces—currently only 40% of the force is dentally ready to deploy—truly herculean efforts must be applied by our units once a unit is alerted. Dental activities compete for the time of leaders, Soldiers, and families as a unit prepares to go to war. Soldiers that are cross-leveled to a ready unit dilute that unit's readiness and lengthen training timelines.

In order to improve the baseline readiness of the Reserve Armed Forces, the same programs, policies, and procedures that have been used to successfully prepare these BCUs need to be applied to our force as a whole.

Actions Taken

The Reserve Armed Forces, in conjunction with the Office of the Surgeon General and the Armed Forces Dental Command, has developed a multifaceted plan that has been approved by both the Army and Reserve Armed Forces leadership.

The cornerstone of this plan is the ability to provide dental treatment to our Soldiers outside of alert.

. . .

The Armed Forces Selected Reserve Dental Readiness Program (SRDRP) will enable units to provide dental treatment to soldiers through local contracts or utilizing the Reserve Health Readiness Program (RHRP).

The Reserve Armed Forces is a true reflection of our nation, and very few of our Citizen-Soldiers have private dental insurance. The participation rate in the TRICARE Reserve Dental Program has hit a plateau at 8%. The ability to provide treatment to our soldiers through the Armed Forces Selected Reserve Dental Readiness Program will have a tremendous impact on the readiness of the Reserve Armed Forces.

This program will also enable the Reserve Armed Forces to maximize the benefits of the Armed Forces Dental Command's initiatives.

. . .

With treatment programs in place, we must also address barriers to compliance with readiness requirements. Active component soldiers do not take unpaid leave to go to the dentist, nor should a Reserve Armed Forces soldier. The ability to provide two medical readiness days per soldier would be a powerful incentive for the soldier to complete readiness requirements, as well as a tool for our commanders to ensure compliance.

. . .

In addition to treatment and incentives, there must be enforcement as recommended by the Commission on Reserve Affairs. As alerted units prepare to go overseas, dental readiness is consistently the main reason for soldier ineligibility for deployment. The Armed Forces have multiple systems which provide unit and senior leaders the capability to track a unit's progress as they prepare for deployment. . . . These tools must be applied and dental readiness enforced by leaders at all levels throughout the Reserve Armed Forces to improve the readiness of our soldiers.

Lastly, in order to execute these programs and sustain an increase in the dental readiness of the Reserve Armed Forces, we must have the appropriate staffing. The Reserve Armed Forces dental corps is currently less than 70% strength, and the majority of remaining providers are eligible for retirement. This committee is considering the Department of Defense's request to increase the retirement age of Reserve Armed Forces health-care providers from age 65 to age 69. This would create the same standard for all three components of service. I would ask that this committee support that request and make that adjustment to the law.

. . .

Likewise, as a reserve component consisting largely of part-time warriors, the Reserve Armed Forces relies heavily on its cadre of full-time personnel to do the administration, maintenance, and training preparation required to produce a ready force. The president's budget request currently before Congress seeks an increase in the level of full-time manning in our force. This is critical. We urge Congress to support this increase.

Conclusion

This is a very exciting time to be in the Reserve Armed Forces. We have deployed over 300,000 dentally ready soldiers in support of the nation since September 11th, 2001. Even so, we can do better. The Army and the Reserve Armed Forces are committed to our Citizen-Soldiers, by caring for them and improving their dental readiness.

I am grateful for this opportunity to appear before this subcommittee and look forward to answering your questions.

➤ WHAT THIS EXAMPLE SHOWS. The testimony writer's consideration of semantics, or word meanings, is noteworthy. "It is surprising how easily the right words can improve understanding and the wrong ones can mire us in confusion" (Bardach, p. 133). Sensitivity to politics surrounding Reserve Armed Forces health care in general, and dental care in particular, is shown here by careful word choice, such as "dental readiness" and "successfully managed transition" and "tremendous improvement." These wordings characterize achievement under difficult working conditions. Careful choice of organization is also evident. The testimony is organized narratively to tell a story of good management in a trying situation. These presentation techniques, deliberate word choice and storytelling, are not deceptive. They are not spin. Rather, they are ethical and rhetorically effective ways to characterize the organization's definition of the problem and message. Implications fit explicit statement well here. The example illustrates care for the interpretation of policy language. When words that have multiple meanings are used, the intended meaning is made clear in context. This writer knows that words influence perception and action. "Political fights are conducted with money, with rules, with votes, and with favors, to be sure, but they are conducted above all with words and ideas" (Stone, p. 36).

The condensed version (shown here) of this testimony likely could be read aloud in five minutes, depending on the presenter's speaking rate. Generally, a page of double-spaced text requires one and a half to two minutes for oral presentation. Witnesses are typically given a 5-minute limit. If the limit were unexpectedly reduced to 1 minute, the presenter of this statement would need to quickly identify a summary paragraph to read. He would be better prepared if, as advised earlier in this chapter, prior to the hearing he had distilled his message into one or two written sentences that he could say easily. He could speak them in 1 minute or less, then await questioning to provide more details in his answers.

Example 2

Scenario

A rural county of a southeastern state has a dwindling population living in or near small, scattered towns. The historically agricultural region is characterized by diminishing wooded wetlands near rivers, large commodity crop farms, corporately owned industrial livestock farms, and meat-processing facilities. Farming, meatpacking, a state prison system, a public school district, and service facilities along the region's only major highway offer low-wage employment. There is little to encourage many residents to stay, former residents to return, and developers to come.

In response to these conditions, a significant number of the county's African American residents have become community advocates and political activists. Postwar migration in the 1940s and 1950s motivated by New Deal agriculture policy and federally subsidized mortgages for affordable land and homes brought urban families to take up farming this rural area. Successful African American farmers achieved rural electrification, farm financing parity, voting rights equity, community-based schools, community centers, and businesses unrelated to farming.

A descendant of these leaders entered postgraduate training to become an attorney. In the University of the District of Columbia David A. Clarke School of Law, he acted as student attorney to meet clients' varied needs for legal assistance. With other student witnesses, he testified in a district council public hearing about conditions in district public housing.

Between semesters, he interned for the nonprofit Rural Coalition with headquarters in the district. As a legal fellow of the coalition representing U.S. and Mexico farmworker organizations and indigenous communities, he developed congressional hearing testimony on various topics. For the example shown here, he coordinated staff contributions and editorial assistance to produce the Coalition statement for the record of a hearing on reform of the Voting Rights Act.

Statement of
Gary R. Redding, Legal Fellow
On behalf
of the Rural Coalition
for The United States Senate Committee on the Judiciary

For inclusion in the record for the hearing entitled,
"From Selma to Shelby County: Working Together to Restore the Protections of the Voting Rights Act"

Washington, D.C.
July 24, 2013
Assuring Voting Rights for Rural and Farm Communities

For forty-eight years, the Voting Rights Act has been a historic law benefitting the masses of U.S. citizens in their quest to participate equally in America's democratic political process. The current and potential threats to citizens' voting rights inform us that the Act is necessary even today. We must now modernize the Act to reflect the realities of today's political landscape. This statement provides a brief overview of past and present voting conditions and limitations in rural and farm communities and the implications of Section 2 of the Voting Rights Act in the wake of the Shelby County, Alabama v. Holder U.S. Supreme Court decision. Our statement provides conclusions and recommendations for updating Section 4 of the Voting Rights Act and making the process for reporting voting rights violations more straightforward and practical.

The Voting Rights Act, a codification of the Fifteenth Amendment to the U.S. Constitution, prohibits states from requiring any "voting qualification or prerequisite to voting, or standard, practice, or procedure . . . to deny or abridge the right of any citizen of the United States to vote on account of race or color" 42 U.S.C. § 1973(a) . . . Thanks to workers in the Civil Rights Movement and citizens particularly in rural communities, many of whom are still active in the Rural Coalition, the Voting Rights Act was enacted in 1965 and has been continually reauthorized, most recently in 2006.

Yet in 2013, many residents in rural and farm communities across America continue to face many of the voting challenges in local, state, and national elections that people in 1965 faced when the Voting Rights Act was passed. Even today, a high percentage of people remain who have difficulty acquiring information about the candidates and the issues. Factors that impede their participation include poor and oftentimes still segregated education systems that have left them unable to fully read and comprehend information about candidates and issues. Lack of access to electricity, computers, and the Internet in their homes and communities also limits their ability to follow news, watch political debates, and otherwise acquire critical information. Senior citizens, especially, still struggle to find transportation to and from voting precincts, which can sometimes be thirty or more miles away from their rural homes. Furthermore, the political process that is supposed to promote voter turnout often discourages or prevents people from voting.

In 1993, the U.S. Congress enacted the National Voter Registration Act (NVRA) to make voting more convenient and accessible by providing a NVRA form for prospective voters to register to vote, update their registration information, or register with a particular political party.

. . .

Despite these federal provisions and protections, proponents of restrictive voting requirements at the state level have in recent times proposed numerous laws to make voting even more difficult. Though each state differs in the particulars, the overall effect reduces voter participation.

Opponents of these restrictive voting requirements and others also argue that they disproportionately target communities of color, the elderly, and youth.

. . .

In addition to . . . widespread attempts to weaken federal voting rights protections with new or excessive requirements and restrictions, some states are trying to nullify it altogether. Shelby County, Alabama v. Holder is the most recent case to come before the Supreme Court. Shelby County, a mostly white suburb of Birmingham, sought to invalidate Sections 4 and 5 of the 1965 Voting Rights Act by claiming they were being punished unfairly for decades old discrimination. Section 5 requires all or parts of sixteen states with a history of racial discrimination in voting to get federal approval before implementing changes to their voting laws . . . Shelby County argued that Sections 4 and 5 should be discontinued because [the County's] current political conditions are no longer racially discriminatory.

. . .

Reporting on voting rights violations poses special challenges for the estimated "46.2 million people, or 15 percent of the U.S. population, [who] reside in rural counties." Hope Yen and Hannah Dreier, Census: Rural US loses population for the first time, Yahoo News (June 13, 2013), http://news.yahoo.com/census-rural-us-loses-population-first-time -040425697.html.

The following hypothetical situation is based on a composite of actual experience encountered by our members in rural communities. It features Larry and is used to illustrate the barriers and challenges to voting faced by people who live in rural communities, and the impact on someone who is denied his rightful chance to vote.

Larry, 38 years old, married, father of ten-year-old twin boys, and a minimum wage factory worker, drives with his family twenty-five miles from his rural community to his polling place to vote. On the way, Larry stops for gas and pays $3.67 a gallon for regular unleaded gas, the current national gas average. After paying $25 for gas for only 6.81 gallons, the family proceeds to the polling place.

It is now 10:00 AM. Larry and his wife decide to each take a child into their respective voting booths. His wife goes into hers but before Larry can make it to his, a poll worker stops him. The poll worker tells Larry that his name is not on the voter roll. Unbeknownst to him, his name had been removed because his voter identification card was returned as undeliverable (as happened and was ruled unconstitutional in U.S. Student Ass'n Found. et al. v. Land et al.). Larry and his wife registered to vote last year during a door-to-door registration drive in their rural community.

Unable to vote or convince the poll worker that he is eligible to vote even though his wife was able to, Larry and his family return home, having driven fifty miles round-trip, only to have one of two votes counted for the family.

Larry and his wife sit at the kitchen table and ponder what to do. They are unaware that a Section 2 complaint can be filed with the United States Department of Justice. The United States Department of Justice's website instructs people to "contact the Voting Section at Voting.Section @usdoj.gov to make a complaint concerning a voting matter." The "Voting.Section@usdoj.gov" link is an email address. Even if they were aware, they could not send the email from their home.

The rural area Larry's family lives in does not have Internet access. Why?

National private cable providers are either refusing to provide Internet service to rural areas or planning to install it for one or two roads a year. . . . Some communities have attempted to establish their own public Internet companies and have seen their efforts thwarted or complicated by cable companies working in tandem with state legislatures. . . . Rural communities who want to build an infrastructure themselves cannot or will be hindered by the law's geographical or rate restrictions.

A few hours later, Larry and his wife try to recall a local community citizen's organization that could possibly help but one does not exist in their community. It is now 2 PM and both have to work in the morning at the local factory, so they scratch the idea of driving to an organization in a neighboring county. Besides, it would require more gas to drive the sixty miles to reach the organization's office.

His wife suggests they call a neighbor who lives two miles away and has dial-up Internet or travel twenty-five miles to the closest library. They decide to call the neighbor and Larry is invited over. Larry sits down at the computer and the dial-up connection fails to connect. The neighbor tells Larry to give it five or so minutes and the connection is slow.

Once online, Larry doesn't know where to go.

If Larry did, he would have to go to http://justice.gov/ or use a search engine to find the site. Once there, he would have to first find on the homepage where the link to "submit a complaint" is under the "Department of Justice Action Center" section. Second, he would have to know to click on the link. Third, he would have to scroll down to find the "voting rights discrimination" link and know to click on it. Fourth, he would come to a page titled "How to File a Complaint" and either click on the "Voting Section" link at the top of the page or have to scroll down to the very bottom to find the "Voting" section. Fifth, Larry would read that he "can register a complaint [by sending] an email message to the Voting Section at Voting.Section@usdoj.gov." Even for a computer savvy person, successfully completing all these steps might prove to be daunting.

Let's say that Larry completed all the aforementioned steps. Larry may see the word "complaint" and believe he is unprepared to compose a formal email explaining why he was denied the right to vote. Furthermore, he may not have an email address because it hasn't made sense to have one since he does not have Internet access at home and therefore no computer.

So, Larry heads back home. It is now 5:00 PM.

Larry decides to call a local attorney to ask for assistance in filing a complaint. The attorney's office is thirty-five miles away and his law firm specializes in local civil and criminal law, not civil rights law. Despite this fact, the attorney invites Larry to his office but informs him that he will be charged $75.00 an hour for the consultation and drafting of the complaint.

Larry gives up. He also decided not to vote in the local school board election that occurred ten days later.

These are typical situations faced by our diverse rural, farm member communities in rural areas around the country.

Although Chief Justice Roberts acknowledged in Shelby that "voting discrimination still exists; no one doubts that," some members of Congress appear to be against working in a bipartisan effort to update the Voting Rights Act. Holder, 133 S. Ct. at 2620. Senate Minority Leader Mitch McConnell (R-KY) called the Voting Rights Act "an important bill that passed back in the '60s at a time when we had a very different America than we have today." Susan Davis, Congress unlikely to act on voting rights ruling, USA Today (June 25, 2013), http://usatoday.com/story/news/politics/2013/06/25/congress-reacts-voting-rights-rulling/2456477/. Rep. Goodlatte (R-VA), chairman of the U.S. House Judiciary Committee, said that even though Section 4 has been ruled unconstitutional, "it's important to note that under the Supreme Court's decision in Shelby County (v. Holder) other very important provisions of the Voting Rights Act remain in place, including Sections 2 and 3." Tom Curry, Conservatives not keen on effort to revise key section of Voting Rights Act, NBCNews (July 18, 2013), http://nbcpolitics.nbcnews.com/_news/2013/07/18/19540938-conservatives-not-keen-on-effort-to-revise-key-section-of-voting-rights-act?lite. Section 3 also requires judicial intervention to impose preclearance requirements on a jurisdiction that enacts discriminatory voting procedures or laws. What Sen. McConnell, Rep. Goodlatte, and others fail to consider, however, are the geographical distinctions that create different challenges for voters in urban and rural areas.

. . .

Conclusions and Recommendations

. . . Below are some of our recommendations and we urge the committee to seek additional input and work quickly to renew this important section of the law.

A new preclearance formula for Section 4 of the Voting Rights Act should be created by the U.S. Congress. . . .

Section 4 should mandate that citizens who believe their voting rights have been violated based on race, age or other factors, may file a petition either on paper or online, and the U.S. Department of Justice should be required to invoke preclearance based on the receipt of such petition . . . .

The U.S. Department of Justice should create an ombudsman position to solely investigate and address complaints of maladministration or voting rights violations. . . .

A "Voter Bill of Rights" should be created and posted in all registrars' offices and in each polling place that includes what a citizen can do if he or she is denied the right to vote. . . .

The U.S. Department of Justice should keep records of the locations from which all complaints, whether by phone, mail or electronically, and be mandated to investigate and invoke preclearance in areas where complaints exceed a set level that should be specified in the revision of the law. . . .

◀━ **WHAT THIS EXAMPLE SHOWS.** This testimony exemplifies "actionable realism" (Wagenaar, p. 278). When defining the problem, the statement keeps in view the real conditions or the "life-world of everyday" (Wagenaar, p. 296). As the testimony's author remarked elsewhere "Hearings usually feature experts or scholars, not the people experiencing the problem first-hand" (Redding).

Larry's story symbolically brings policy-affected people into the hearing. His experience illustrates the needs for action.

The example shows the "normative leap" from description to prescription (Stone, p. 171). For instance, Larry's difficulty with reporting a voting rights violation via the Internet can be restated as a premise: rural communities lack adequate Internet service. The premise leads to the conclusion that rural access to communication technology must be remedied if voting rights are to be protected. That conclusion leads to recommendation of policy action to create an ombudsman position with capability of 24-hour Election Day violations reporting by telephone or by mail.

Skillfully using creative writing techniques and qualitative evidence to represent a policy problem for a policy maker audience, this testimony meets two criteria of effective policy communication, credibility and usefulness. *Tip:* To connect a need, relevant data, and a recommendation, think narratively. You might tell a story to show why action is needed and what action to take. Keep analysis close to the empirical evidence of causal conditions revealed by the story. Fit recommendations to the storyline.

Storytelling might not be appropriate in all policy communication genres. Policy memos, for instance, might not include an explicit story. However, policy memos might be narratively organized. They might have a storyline to show change or progression or simply to move readers' attention along.

Another strength of the statement in Example 2 is its handling of complexity. Policy problems are always complex. Complexity can be internal intricacy or the number of moving parts and part-whole relationships in a problem. Interdependencies between policy problems also create complexity (Roe, p. 2). This statement exposes a previously unrecognized moving part in the problem of voting rights, inadequate Internet service and access. The testimony's analysis highlights a neglected equity concern (Wolf). Identification of unequal Internet access brings the interdependency of voting rights and communication infrastructure into view. The interdependency adds a new dimension to the race-based narrative of voting rights inequity and more specificity to recognized geographic, economic, and infrastructural disparities.

Any policy communication is necessarily selective. Writers selectively represent the intricacies of a topic in accord with a viewpoint and a message. In Example 2, the writer's viewpoint, message, and selective representation explicitly disrupt taken-for-granted understandings, support the message that the Supreme Court ruling got it wrong, and recommend corrections of the Court's mistake. As a subpoint, the writer challenges the assumptions of experts and analysts who take Internet access for granted. He makes clear that access is unevenly available. He asks the Senate Judiciary Committee, which has power to create federal Internet policies and administration, to recognize geographic and economic factors in Internet access.

Particularly in rural areas, poverty-affected populations are disadvantaged by limited access.

The written statement in Example 2 is intended for submission to the printed hearing record. It could not be read aloud during the hearing itself because it is too long and too densely detailed. To prepare this statement for oral delivery, a witness would follow guidance presented earlier in this chapter to have ready 2 summaries, a 1-minute message without details and a 5-minute summary with key details. The witness would also anticipate questions and answers and prepare notes on how to answer them.

Takeaway and Look Ahead

Testimony in a public hearing is a highly visible way of getting your knowledge, perspective, and message into legislative action and onto the public record. This chapter alerts you to differences between writing for silent reading and writing for oral presentation. Policy communicators must know how to do both. Chapter 10, next, introduces another important way of influencing policy, submitting written public comment during administrative rule making.

Exercise

Observe Communication Dynamics in a Public Hearing

Examples of written testimony can be found on the websites of respected nonprofit organizations, public policy institutes, some government agencies, and congressional committees. For consistently good examples that meet standards advocated by this guide, see U.S. Government Accountability Office Reports and Testimonies (http://gao.gov/).

To observe face to face interaction in a hearing, especially to understand the importance of questions and answers, view recorded congressional committee hearings on committee websites. Or, while a hearing is in progress, view it live on the cable news channel C-SPAN 3.

Read the written testimony statements posted on the website of the committee holding the hearing. Compare the written and spoken versions of testimony. How did the witness utilize the written statement when speaking? What features of the written statement were easy or hard to deliver orally? How did questions and answers elaborate the written statement?

References

Bardach, E. (2011). Semantic tips: A summary. In *A practical guide for policy analysis: The eightfold path to more effective problem solving* (Appendix C, 4th ed.). Washington, DC: CQ Press.

Redding, G. (2014). Personal correspondence.

Roe, Emery. (1994). *Narrative policy analysis: Theory and practice.* Durham, NC: Duke University Press.

Smith, C. F. (1993). "Is it worth fixing this plane?" The rhetorical life of information in a congressional oversight hearing on the B-1 bomber. In B. Sims (Ed.), *Studies in technical communication: Selected papers of the 1992 CCCC and NCTE conferences* (pp. 111–146). Denton, TX: University of North Texas Press.

Stone, D. (2012). *Policy paradox: The art of political decision making* (3rd ed.). New York, NY: W. W. Norton. Cited in Schon, D. (1980), "Generative metaphor: A perspective on problem setting in public policy." In A. Ortony (Ed.), *Metaphor and thought.* Cambridge, UK: Cambridge University Press.

Wagenaar, H. (2011). *Meaning in action: Interpretation and dialogue in policy analysis.* Armonk, NY: Sharpe.

Wolf, Charles Jr. (1980). *Ethics and policy analysis.* Santa Monica CA: Rand Paper Series P-6463-2.

CHAPTER 10

Public Comment:
Influence Administration

Overview

Formal public comment gives everyone a say in public policy making. Anyone can write a formal comment when a government agency calls for it. This chapter prepares you to write a formal comment that is likely to be taken seriously by the requesting agency. Samples illustrate comments using legal argument (Example 1), technical analysis (Examples 2, 3), and civic activism (Example 4). A discussion topic helps you to frame a comment. Exercises offer practice in writing comments. Adding to your know-how, this chapter introduces federal plain language guidelines to supplement "Writing Clearly" (Appendix).

＊ ＊ ＊

The Administrative Procedures Act as well as other laws and executive orders require federal agencies to seek public comment during rule making on proposed standards and regulations. Do public comments make a difference? Yes. Agencies regularly pull back a proposed rule for revision based on comments received. Do carefully prepared formal comments make a bigger difference than mass emails or form letters? Yes. Agencies review substantive comments more closely than others. Does the method of delivery matter? Yes. Written comments are reviewed, whether submitted electronically or mailed. Telephoned or emailed responses to formal calls for comment are not reviewed.

What happens after written comments are submitted? Agency-contracted external reviewers who are specialists in the subject matter read each comment. For instance, air quality specialists at the Research Triangle Institute (RTI) in North Carolina review Environmental Protection Agency (EPA) public comments on air quality regulation. Comments might number a million or more. In a human process minimally assisted by information management software, reviewers first sort comments into categories such as general opposition or support, substantive, or out of scope. The majority (95%) of comments goes into general opposition or support. Comments that simply support another ("incorporate by reference") and duplicate comments go into opposition or support. A minority goes into out of scope.

The remaining substantive comments are read line by line. Reviewers fit substantive contents to an outline derived from the call's preamble; sections of the proposed rule; the agency's questions stating what it wants to learn from public comments; statutory and executive orders that relate to the call, and agency remarks on changes in the rule language. The outline evolves if review shows that more or different sections are needed.

Within the substantive category, comments are clustered by topic. Comments that offer new, unexpected, or should-be-considered information are flagged. Clusters are summarized and synthesized by the RTI reviewer before passing them on to a technical expert at RTI or in EPA to confirm accuracy. Finally reviewers, sometimes in collaboration with agency experts, draft recommendations based on comment patterns and specifics. Overall, the process of reviewing public comments at RTI is iterative, shared, and human-performed. It is not automated (Bullock). Probably, this is typical of current public comment review. However, some federal agencies are experimenting with digital rule making or e-rule making to include computer-aided analysis of public comments (Schlosberg et al; Shulman et al.).

Agencies have discretion in using comments for rule modification and in describing the use they might have made. In the milk-labeling case (Chapter 1) the Bureau of Food Safety and Laboratory Services of the Pennsylvania Department of Agriculture (PDA) described a modification this way:

"PDA has received a great deal of input on the standards set forth in [the new standard on milk labeling announced on

October 24, 2007]. . . . We are now in a position to inform you further as to the results of reviewing the input we received. Enclosed please find a new document titled "Revised Standards and Procedures for the Approval of Proposed Labeling of Fluid Milk" dated January 17, 2008. ". . . Please review this document carefully and govern yourself accordingly."

Public comment is routinely sought in federal rule making, but not for state rule making. However, states must seek public comment in regulatory procedures for granting, revoking, or renewing permits for activities that affect public life. To illustrate, comments on a Pennsylvania mining permit modification are shown in Examples 3 and 4, this chapter.

Regrettably, few citizens know about this opportunity to have influence. Few engage opportunities to submit formal comments on proposed administrative policy. As a result, narrowly interested groups dominate the rule making process. That is not what agencies want. Agencies want broad participation. Regulators want to get it right. Federal, state, and local agencies welcome any type of comment that can help them make and justify their decisions. A comment might be a technical analysis, a philosophical argument, an opinion based on personal experience, advocacy, or a request to hold a public meeting on the proposed action. A simple letter can have impact. Responsible agencies take seriously any well-prepared comment, especially any that suggests realistic and feasible alternatives.

Public comment is important because administrative public policy broadly affects present and future life. The more comments, the better the likelihood of good government (http://regulations.gov/).

How to Write a Public Comment

Goal: Your participation in making the rules for enacting and enforcing law.

Scope: Limited to the specific proposed administrative action.

Strategy: Base comments on your authority to respond. Personal experience, organizational advocacy, vocational or professional background, or specialized knowledge are all useful.

Product: Formal written comment.

Communication objective: To influence the administration of a law.

Task 1: Find Calls for Public Comment

Federal Sources

The U.S. government's official source for notifications of proposed rule making is the *Federal Register*, published daily. You can find the *Federal Register* either in government information depository libraries or online at http://federalregister.gov/. Look for "Proposed Rules" or "Notices." Look for announcements by agencies authorized to act on topics of concern to you.

If you already know the executive branch department, and within it the relevant agency that administers laws in your area of concern, do not go initially to the Register. Go to the website of the relevant department (the Department of Transportation, for instance) and find the relevant agency (National Highway Traffic Safety Administration, for instance).

Or, go to the website of an advocacy group associated with your concern. Browsing there is likely to turn up the name of both the department and the agency. Sign up for the group's email action alerts.

State Sources

If you are concerned about a state issue, you can find calls for public comment in state administration notifications such as the Pennsylvania Bulletin or the New York State Register. Every state has such a publication. Or, if you know the relevant state agency for your concern, go to its website. Or go to the websites of advocacy groups for your concern.

Local Sources

For local government matters, watch the Public Notices section of the newspaper of record. Local governments typically designate (by geographic region or by population size) one or more widely-read local newspapers as a newspaper of record. Calls for public comment on local government are published there. Notices might be also posted in local government offices or, possibly, on their websites.

Task 2: Write a Public Comment

In most respects, writing a public comment is like writing any other policy document. The demands for preparation and planning are the same. The same expectations for clarity, credibility, and conciseness apply. One possible difference: some calls for public input specify the exact information needed. If the call to which you are responding requests specific content, provide it. If you have additional information, include it but not at the expense of requested contents.

> To help ensure that your comment will be taken seriously, aim for the following features and qualities:
>
> • Narrow focus
> • Evidence, analyses, and references supporting your view
> • Indication of public support of your view
> • Positive and feasible alternatives
> • Easily understood or plain language.
>
> Before you write, use the Method (Chapter 2) to plan. After you write, check the document against the standards (Checklists, Chapter 2).

Four Examples

Examples 1 and 2 illustrate rule making by federal agencies. Examples 3 and 4 illustrate permitting by a state agency. Comments by nonprofit organizations (Examples 1 and 3), experts (Example 2), and community leaders (Example 4) are shown. Scenarios provide context for each example.

Example 1

Scenario

At the nonprofit National Farmer's Union (NFU) headquarters in Washington, DC, a government relations specialist new on the job is assigned to write a formal public comment. His product will be the NFU's submission in response to an Environmental Protection Agency (EPA) call for comments on a proposed rule to make clear "which water bodies are protected under the Clean Water Act" (EPA-HQ-OW 2011-0880://regulations.gov/). He has relevant prior experience as a public affairs communicator for news clip services, blogs, and farming publications as well as legal writing experience as law student intern for the EPA. But he has not previously written a formal comment.

He faces a tight deadline for responding to EPA's call. On advice of the NFU's board president and policy director, he first consults the organization's current policy manual (https://nfu.org/2015/04/17/nfu-2015-policy/). Two policy positions under Article VI, "Water and Land Policy," state the NFU's opposition to extending the Clean Water Act's jurisdiction and its support for environmental stewardship. Those positions become his guidelines. Next he consults practical experts, NFU farmers in western states, particularly South and North Dakota, who are most likely to be affected by administrative change in the Clean Water Act. As he drafts, he interacts continually with farmers, NFU state and regional chapter presidents, and NFU members who contact him.

Through his interactions, he encounters polarized opinion, partisan politics, and misinformation about the proposed rule. This surprises him because he knows the NFU to be deliberative in its policy considerations (Example 3, Chapter 8). He attributes the unexpected discord to NFU's late entry into an already compromised public discourse. Well-funded industry groups, some in agriculture, came together early to loudly convey a single negative message, stop the rule. "Ditch the Rule" advocates include the National Association of State Departments of Agriculture, American Farm Bureau Federation, National Cattlemen's Beef Association, and others. Despite the EPA's issuance of an interpretation specifying fifty-six exemptions for conservation and farming practice in addition to traditional exemptions in the proposed rule, the negative public relations campaign has fueled anti-government convictions.

Rather than simply opposing the rule, NFU's choice is to offer advice to EPA on how to secure a rule that works for family agriculture. The choice is nuanced, hard to build consensus around, and hard to represent.

After three weeks of intensive drafting and revision, the writer submits NFU's comment ahead of deadline. Subsequently, National Public Radio and local radio stations interview him about the union's position. His experience shows that procedural submission to an administrative agency's formal call is not the end of the assignment. Communicators might need media skills for follow-up, too.

September 22, 2014

Water Docket
Environmental Protection Agency
Mail Code: 2822T
1200 Pennsylvania Ave. NW.
Washington, DC 20460
Docket ID No. EPA-HQ-OW-2011-0880

ATTENTION: DOCKET ID NO. EPA-HQ-OW-2011-0880: DEFINITION OF "WATERS OF THE UNITED STATES UNDER THE CLEAN WATER ACT"

Dear Administrator McCarthy and Lieutenant General Bostick:

National Farmers Union (NFU) welcomes the opportunity to submit comments to the Environmental Protection Agency (EPA) and the U.S. Army Corps of Engineers (Corps) on the proposed rule regarding the definition of "waters of the United States" under the Clean Water Act (CWA). As this rulemaking process continues, NFU may submit additional comments.

Since 1902, NFU has advocated for the economic and social well-being and quality of life of family farmers and their communities through the sustainable production of food, fiber, feed and fuel. NFU represents nearly 200,000 members nationwide, with members in all 50 states and organized divisions in 33 states. NFU is a federation of state and regional organizations.

Clean water is vital to the productivity and well-being of America's farms, ranches and rural communities. The CWA seeks to "restore and maintain the chemical, physical, and biological integrity of the Nation's waters. NFU's members understand the importance of respecting clean water as a shared resource and believe the integrity of the nation's water can be protected without unnecessarily encumbering the activities of the regulated community. NFU's policy, enacted annually by delegates to the organization's national convention, opposes broadening the definition of what waters are considered jurisdictional and supports the uniform administration of EPA policies nationwide.

The EPA and Corps' (agencies) stated goal for the proposed rule is to improve protection of public health and water resources while increasing certainty for the regulated community and reducing troublesome and costly litigation. Protecting the nation's water resources is a complicated matter, and so by necessity are the CWA and any rule implementing it. This topic requires careful consideration and measured discourse over the legitimate concerns facing the regulated community.

. . .

It is not satisfactorily clear whether the proposed rule, in its present form, would implement policies that NFU supports. However, NFU's members recognize the agencies' rulemaking process on this matter as an opportunity to achieve their policy goals because the current regulatory landscape allows for inconsistent determinations that expand the CWA's definition of jurisdictional waters. The purpose of the following comments is to provide the agencies with advice for drafting a final rule that does not increase CWA jurisdiction and promotes consistent application of EPA policies, which aligns with the agencies' stated intent. NFU will oppose a rule that does not respect these critical components of the organization's policy. These comments will help the agencies avoid language that, even when drafted in good faith, could be taken out of context and used to stretch CWA jurisdiction in the future.

. . .

Proposed Definition of "waters of the United States."

"Tributary"

The CWA establishes the agencies' permitting jurisdiction over specifically listed waters. Paragraphs (a)(1)–(a)(5) of the proposed rule restate well-settled tenets of the agencies' jurisdiction under the CWA and do not warrant further comment. However, section (a)(5)'s inclusion of "All tributaries of waters identified in paragraphs (a)(1) through (4) of this section" warrants examination. This language has invoked significant concern in the regulated community that the proposed rule would increase the jurisdictional reach of the CWA. The agencies should address this concern and confirm this language does not increase jurisdiction by incorporating the following points in the final rule.

. . .

The preamble . . . notes that the proposed rule sets forth, for the first time, a regulatory definition of "tributary." The proposed rule defines "tributary" as "a water physically characterized by the presence of a bed and banks and ordinary high water mark . . . which contributes flow, either directly or through another water, to a water identified in paragraphs (a) (1) through (4) of this section." In order to provide more clarity to the regulated community, the agencies should note in the final rule that these features take years to form. This should mitigate concern that temporary accumulations directly related to isolated rain events will be considered jurisdictional. The agencies should add further clarifying language, including but not limited to descriptive examples of water and events that are not considered tributaries, in the final rule in order to ensure these distinctions are well-understood in the regulated community.

. . .

"Adjacent"

The proposed rule would change section (a)(6) from an articulation of the CWA's jurisdiction over wetlands adjacent to "waters of the United States" to an explanation of the CWA's jurisdiction over "All waters, including wetlands, adjacent to" waters identified in (a)(1) to (a)(5) as jurisdictional.

As with the definition of "tributary" discussed above, this change is causing apprehension among the regulated community. The agencies should consider the following points in drafting the final rule to make clear that this change does not expand jurisdiction.

The proposed rule defines "adjacent" as "bordering, contiguous or neighboring" at (c)(1). It notes further that "Waters, including wetlands, separated from other waters of the United States by man-made dikes or barriers, natural river berms, beach dunes and the like are 'adjacent waters.'"

The jurisdictional reach of "adjacent waters," then, is largely dependent on the definition of "neighboring." This proposed rule defines "neighboring" for the first time. The preamble notes that the term is currently applied broadly, but the proposed rule defines "neighboring" as "waters located within the riparian area or floodplain of a water identified in (a) (1) through (5) of this section, or waters with a shallow subsurface hydrological connection or confined surface hydrologic connection to such a jurisdictional water."

. . .

The preamble also asks for specific comment "on whether the rule text should provide greater specificity with regard to how the agencies will determine if a water is located in the floodplain of a jurisdictional water." The agencies should uniformly use a 20 year flood interval zone when evaluating these waters. . . The agencies should also provide clarity to the regulated community by stating in the final rule, "mere proximity to a jurisdictional water is not cause for a determination that a water is jurisdictional as 'neighboring' or 'adjacent,' and a scientifically-verifiable, substantial surface connection must be present for any water outside a floodplain or riparian zone to be found jurisdictional."

"Significant Nexus"
Other waters not covered by the above-discussed jurisdictional categories may fall within the CWA's jurisdiction if a case-by-case determination is made finding the water has a "significant nexus" with a water identified in sections (a)(1) through (3).

The proposed rule at section (c)(7) says "The term significant nexus means that a water, including wetlands, either alone or in combination with other similarly situated waters in the region (i.e., the watershed that drains to the nearest water identified in paragraphs (a)(1) through (3) of this section), significantly affects the chemical, physical, or biological integrity of a water identified in paragraphs (a)(1) through (3) of this section." The proposed rule also states "Other waters, including wetlands, are similarly situated when they perform similar functions and are located sufficiently close together or sufficiently close to a 'water of the United

States' so that they can be evaluated as a single landscape unit with regard to their effect on the chemical, physical, or biological integrity of a water identified in paragraphs (a)(1) through (a)(3) of this section."

. . .

The term "similarly situated" must be examined, since it allows the agencies to consider multiple waters together in making "significant nexus" determinations. The prerequisite condition for "other waters" to be considered "similarly situated," before any assessment of geographic proximity to additional "other waters" or jurisdictional waters, is performance of similar functions. The preamble further explains that a "similarly situated" determination requires an evaluation of whether waters in a region "can reasonably be expected to function together in their effect on the chemical, physical, or biological integrity of downstream traditional navigable waters, interstate waters, or the territorial seas," and whether waters are "sufficiently close" to each other or a jurisdictional water.

The description of "similarly situated" waters above includes so many variables that it would be difficult for the regulated community to accurately anticipate the outcome of such a determination, opening the door to increased uncertainty. To give the regulated community more clarity in anticipating the results of "similarly situated" evaluations, the agencies should provide a list of functions that a group of waters must perform together in order to be considered "similarly situated." These functions include affecting the reach and flow of a jurisdictional water and allowing or barring the movement of aquatic species, nutrients, pollutants or sediments to a jurisdictional water.

. . .

This added clarity would ease concerns regarding the rule held by NFU members in the Prairie Pothole Region, in which a farm may be littered with potholes. In many cases, a pothole may be located near a jurisdictional water and have a physical surface connection to that jurisdictional water. Another pothole may be located near to the first pothole and yet have no connection to it. The agencies should assure farmers the second pothole, even though it is near to the first pothole, will not automatically be considered "similarly situated" to the first pothole strictly due to geographic proximity. At the very least, the final rule should clarify that the term "similarly situated," for purposes of determining whether "other waters" maintain a "significant nexus" with jurisdictional waters, is not a simple geographic determination. The agencies should elaborate that "similarly situated" means both waters that are near to each other and sharing an identifiable hydrogeological feature in common. A water would not be considered "similarly situated" due to geographic proximity alone.

. . .

Exemptions for Agricultural Activities

The preamble indicates that the proposed rule does not affect existing regulatory exemptions for agricultural activities. There is nothing in the proposed rule that calls this assertion into question.

. . .

MISCELLANEOUS MATTERS

Shallow Subsurface Hydrologic Connections

. . . Until more scientific evidence is provided, groundwater connections alone should not be used to find non-navigable waters jurisdictional.

. . .

Pesticide Applications

. . . This is not the proper venue for discussing these applications.

. . .

CONCLUSION

NFU understands the agencies' stated goal of enhancing protections for our nation's water resources while providing increased certainty to the regulated community. The comments above reflect NFU's understanding of the proposed rule and explain ways the proposed rule could be improved to more effectively accomplish the agencies' stated goal in the final rule while maintaining conformity with NFU's policy. NFU stands ready to offer further assistance in this regard as the agencies may find helpful. Thank you for your consideration of these comments.

Sincerely,
Roger Johnson
President

(Content and footnotes are omitted because of space limitations. Read NFU's full comment here: http://regulations.gov/ posted 09/24/2014 ID: EPA-HQ-OW-2011-0880-6249)

►◄ WHAT THIS EXAMPLE SHOWS. Administrative public policy directly affects daily life and ordinary activities. Most of us come into contact with public policy less through legislation and more through managing our affairs to comply with standards and regulations that enforce law. For water management, standards and regulations often generate controversy. The stakes are high and effects are far-reaching. Water is critical for all forms of life and many industries.

Consequently, advocates for human activities, the environment, wildlife, and commerce are concerned. In all, over a million individuals and organizations responded to EPA's call in 2014 for comments to define terms of the Clean Water Act.

EPA issues more calls for comment than do other federal agencies except Health and Human Services. EPA's calls often entail controversy. In this example, contention focused on water connectivity, or how one water body relates to another. The agency wanted to define types of connection that would qualify related water bodies for protection under the Clean Water Act. The original act protected only navigable waters such as lakes and rivers. Recent Supreme Court decisions had allowed for protecting other waters "adjacent to" or "similarly situated as" jurisdictional lakes and rivers. However, the court's decisions did not define those and other key terms. After multiple scientific and governmental assessments of the need for a new rule, EPA asked for public comment to help define the terms.

The NFU writer responded with legal argument using plain language and content organization mirroring EPA's call. By referring to EPA's proposed definitions in the order presented, by citing their exact location in the preamble or sections of the rule, then by immediately providing NFU's response, the comment moves efficiently along, point-for-point, to meet EPA's request. (Its organization alerts comment reviewers that it is a substantive comment.) This kind of organization resembles the terms-construction phase of legal proceedings. Extraneous matter is strictly excluded.

Terse expression in plain language (simplified wording) and mostly declaratory (subject-verb-object) sentence construction augment the organization of content.

Tip: Plain language is defined by government communicators as easy to read, understand, and use (http://plainlanguage.gov/). Plain language is reader oriented and works well for complex audiences. It is preferred in communications to government.

Comments submitted to the EPA have a complex audience. Agency staff are primary, with comment reviewers as the agency's filters. Anybody who must comply with the revised rule ("the regulated community") is secondary. The NFU writer correctly assumes that EPA might utilize language offered in public comment when issuing the final rule. For the important secondary audience who must comply with the rules, the writer advises EPA not only on definitions but also on ways to gain farmers' compliance. Here's an instance of complex audience-management by the NFU comment writer: "The agencies should provide further clarity for the regulated community [farmers]. . . by stating in the final rule 'This rule does not require a permit for any plowing and planting activity that was legally conducted without a permit before this rule was issued.'"

A structural feature of plain language is the comment's subheadings that repeat EPA's terms. The repetition makes it easier for reviewers to fit the NFU comment to the outline of EPA's call and to categorize them appropriately for recommendation to EPA.

Another structural feature of plain language is declarative sentence structure using active voice. Most sentences in the NFU comment are declarative in active voice; their subjects do the verb's action. For instance, "NFU [subject] will oppose [verb] a rule that does not respect. . . the organization's policy."

By combining these expressive and structural features, NFU's comment exemplifies good policy communication. It is likely to receive the EPA's respectful attention.

Tip: The website to which formal comments are posted, Regulations.gov, offers excellent do's and don'ts on writing effective comments. Additionally, the Plain Language Action and Information Network (http://plainlanguage.gov) offers excellent instructions on communicating simply and directly.

Special Tip: The government relations specialist who wrote the NFU statement advises you to keep your eye on the *Federal Register*. You could be writing in response to a call for comment tomorrow, ready or not. Keep your other eye on newspaper opinion pages and online interactive blogs in your area of concern. You could be interviewed the day after tomorrow, ready or not.

Example 2

Scenario

A national transportation safety investigative board holds four days of hearings on air bag safety. The board, which reports both to the Congress and to the executive branch, is concerned about the unanticipated high rates of injury from air bag deployment. The witness list for the hearings includes representatives of auto manufacturers, insurance companies, safety institutes, auto safety advocacy groups, air bag manufacturers, and auto parts suppliers. The purpose of the hearings is to enable the board to make recommendations for improving air bag safety.

Based on the board's ensuing recommendations and its own investigations, the federal agency responsible for automotive safety regulations, the National Highway Traffic Safety Administration, announces that it intends to modify the current standard for air bags. The agency announces its proposed modification in the *Federal Register* and calls for public comment.

In response to the call for comments, two experts in automotive safety jointly write a technical comment and submit it in the rule making process. They point out shortcomings in the agency's proposed modification, and they propose an alternative.

COMMENT TO THE DOCKET CONCERNING AMENDMENTS TO FMVSS 208, OCCUPANT CRASH PROTECTION

Summary of Comments

Federal motor vehicle safety standards (FMVSS) must, by law, meet the need for motor vehicle safety. This proposal (Docket No. NHTSA 98–4405; Notice I) purports to meet that need by requiring advanced air bags. In fact, it is primarily written to address the problem of inflation induced injuries and would provide little additional protection.

The worst of the inflation-induced injuries resulted in several hundred fatalities to children and out-of-position adults (including those sitting too close to the steering wheel) and from late, low-speed crash air bag deployments. NHTSA [National Highway Traffic Safety Administration] had assumed that manufacturers would conduct comprehensive air bag testing to ensure that inflation would not inflict injury under reasonable foreseeable conditions. It is arguable (although probably not practical policy) that NHTSA could address inflation-induced injuries under safety defect provisions of the National Traffic and Motor Vehicle Safety Act.

. . .

A key part of this notice proposes two options: (I) tests of air bag systems with dummies in close proximity to ensure that inflation induced injuries are unlikely, or (2) requirements for occupant sensors to ensure that air bags will not inflate if an occupant is in a position where he or she is at risk of injury from the inflating air bag.

In response to the proposed alternatives, we expect manufacturers to choose occupant sensors to prevent air bag inflation for certain occupant situations. This untested sensor technology might actually increase casualties because of inaccurate determinations of occupant risks and degraded reliability from the added complexity.

Experts in the field have suggested a number of potential air bag design and performance features that might reduce inflation induced injuries. The Canadian government and NHTSA deserve credit for their research and analysis in this field despite NHTSA's belated recognition that an official response was necessary. It is not clear which approach would be most effective, or even most cost-effective, but we think it is unlikely that NHTSA's proposed regulation will yield an optimal result.

This notice [of proposal amendments] also fails to address occupant protection challenges involving one to two orders of magnitude more casualties for which feasible technologies are available. These include raising safety belt use to near universality, protection of occupants in rollover crashes, and addressing compatibility problems between passenger cars and light trucks.

Many of these deficiencies can be overcome with a third alternative that retains the simplicity of the original automatic occupant crash protection standard; does not introduce complex, untested occupant sensors; and meets other needs for motor vehicle safety. It depends fundamentally on NHTSA's willingness to propose acceptable, effective inducements for using safety belts.

. . .

A Third Option Would Encourage Belt Use

We are proposing that a third option be added to NHTSA's notice that would ensure safety belt use with acceptable and effective belt use inducements built into the vehicle.

. . .

NHTSA must recognize that the fundamental problem with its occupant restraint policy is that a substantial minority of motorists does not use safety belts. In fact, a much larger proportion of those most likely to be involved in serious crashes drive unbelted. Nearly universal belt use is critical to any rational occupant crash protection program.

. . .

An Alternative to the Proposed Amendment

Our specific proposal is that NHTSA add a third option to its notice on advanced air bags. Under this option:

- A manufacturer must install an effective, but not onerous safety belt use inducement in a new motor vehicle of a type that would be permitted under the "interlock" amendment (15 U.S.C.1410b) to the National Traffic and Motor Vehicle Safety Act.
  . . .

- A motor vehicle must meet comparative injury criteria of FMVSS 208 and in addition [in crashworthiness tests using dummies] there can be no contact between the head of the driver or passenger dummy and any part of the vehicle (other than the air bag or belt restraint system) or any other part of the dummy, in a frontal barrier crash at a speed of up to 35 mph with belted occupants.
  . . .

- Air bags may not deploy under any frontal crash speed barrier impacts below 16 mph.
  . . .

Discussion

Our alternative would provide occupant crash protection that is at least equal in all respects to that provided by the present standard and NCAP consumer information program.

. . .

This proposal would substantially increase belt use and, because of the head impact requirements, would ensure that air bags provide good head protection. Air bags that can meet this criterion would provide some frontal crash protection to the small number of unbelted occupants (who would, of course, be unbelted by their own conscious choice).

If manufacturers would choose our alternative, it would save a minimum of 7000 lives per year compared with the present FMVSS208, making it one of the most cost-effective standards ever.

(The full comment can be found at http://regulations.gov/. See NHTSA-1998–4405–0062. Appendix 1 shows a petition the commenters' additionally submitted. Later, the NHTSA summarizes all comments on its 1998 notice in a preamble to its next published notice on air bag safety. It says how the comments influenced its plans to modify the standard in 1998. In an appendix, NHTSA states its reasons for rejecting the two experts' alternative shown here.)

Example 3

Scenario

A state environmental protection department's bureau of mining, which regulates mineral extraction industries in the state, announces a proposed revision in a mining company's operating permit. In accordance with "sunshine" requirements for permitting processes, the agency publishes the applicant's proposal to mine deeper than its original permit allowed. The mining company is asking the bureau to remove restrictions on the company's operation at a specific site. The primary restriction prohibits mining at levels that might adversely affect local groundwater quantity and quality. The restriction is warranted in a region where well-water supply and quality vary according to groundwater conditions and where high-quality cold-water trout fishing streams are fed by local springs near the mining site.

In response to the bureau's call for public comment on the mine operator's request for permit revision, a local environmental conservation group and a local civic organization write letters of comment (Examples 3 and 4, this chapter). Other interested parties write letters, too, including a national sport fishing group, local businesses dependent on tourism, and individual citizens. At the request of the civic organization, the agency holds a public meeting. The conservation group hires a professional stenographer (who is also a notary public) to transcribe the meeting. In addition, the group invites local news reporters. The meeting is well attended. The bureau officials, the mine operator, and the residents of the region affected by the mine vigorously discuss the request to lift restrictions on the mine. After the meeting, the conservation group provides the transcript to the bureau as a written record of public comment. If administrative litigation regarding this permit ensues, the transcript will provide evidence.

Following the public meeting, an attorney member of the local environmental conservation group, in collaboration with members who are expert in hydrogeology and water quality engineering, writes a technical and legal analysis of the mining company's application for permit modifications. The chair of the group's relevant committee signs and submits the comment. Selections are given here.

TECHNICAL and LEGAL ANALYSIS
July 29, 2001

Michael W. Smith
District Mining Manager
Pennsylvania Department of Environmental Protection
P.O. Box 209 Hawk Run, PA 16840–0209
VIA Hand Delivery'

Re: Con-Stone, Inc's, June 7, 2001, application to revise permit #14920301

Dear Mr. Smith:

The Penns Valley Conservation Association (PVCA) has reviewed Con-Stone, Inc.'s, June 7, 2001, application to revise permit #14920301 to allow removal of the Valentine Limestone below the 1080' elevation. PVCA wishes to work cooperatively with Con-Stone and the Pennsylvania Department of Environmental Protection (DEP) to ensure that mining operations protect the watershed surrounding the Aaronsburg Operation, including Elk and Pine Creeks [state-designated Exceptional Value (EV) streams] and Penns Creek [state-designated High-Quality (HQ) stream]. In that spirit of cooperation, and for protection of those streams, PVCA requests denial of Con-Stone's current application for the following reasons.

1. PVCA recommends retaining special conditions 1, 2, and 4 in Part B, Noncoal Surface Mining Permit No 14920301, Revised July 13, 1999, Special Conditions or Requirements. As District Mining Manager Michael W. Smith said in an August 27, 1999, letter to Con-Stone, "The mining limit of 1080 feet was originally established to keep mining activity out of the average seasonal low water table to minimize the potential for impacts to groundwater and to Spring S-26. We are not convinced that mining below 1080 feet can be accomplished without added risk of water impact."
   . . .

2. To manage the risks of mining below the water table, the proposed amendment calls for phased mining with a progressively deeper penetration of the water table. However, there is a total lack of detail in the permit amendment regarding the specific steps to be taken in the phased mining process. There should be

clear language in the permit that stipulates consecutive mining and reclamation and attaches some time schedule and methodology for data analysis and reporting prior to advancing to the next phase of mining.

3. In PVCA's original discussions with DEP, Mike Smith indicated that Con-Stone would have to develop a new infiltration basin system to dispose of the groundwater pumped from the quarry. The permit amendment is contrary to this position as it utilizes the infiltration galleries currently designated for storm water disposal. PVCA requests that separate infiltration systems covered by separate NPDES permits be developed for the storm water and groundwater pumped from the pit.

4. The materials contained in the permit amendment do not adequately describe the hydrogeologic conditions. An appropriately scaled map showing the current pit location, the water table configuration, the location of all boreholes, the sedimentation basin, and infiltration galleries should be prepared. Without water table contour mapping, it is impossible to address issues such as recirculation of the water pumped from the mine.

5. The May 7–10, 2001, pit pumping test performed by the mine operator provides little useful information regarding the extent of [potential loss of water supply] due to mining operations . . . If DEP is going to grant the requested amendment, PVCA requests a special condition that Con-Stone is responsible for replacing the water supply for any water losses that result from mining operations. . . .

6. . . . In the context of the EV protection of the watershed, a much more comprehensive modeling effort is warranted. "Ideal aquifer" calculations such as those used to calculate inflow to the pit are not applicable in this setting.

7. Monitoring should be expanded, again at Con-Stone's cost, to be more complete by including all biological and chemical monitoring required by DEP's water quality anti-degradation regulations and implementation guidelines.

. . .

10. The permit amendment submission does not appear to be signed and sealed by a licensed professional geologist.

11. PVCA believes Con-Stone must apply for a new or revised NPDES [National Pollution Discharge] permit for the proposed quarry dewatering activities.

. . .

12. PVCA does not believe that Con-Stone has complied with all necessary pre-permit requirements under DEP's water quality anti-degradation regulations and implementation guidelines . . . Further, the application has not sought review by local and county governments to ensure compatibility with applicable regulations, ordinances, and comprehensive plans and to allow government to identify local and regional environmental and economic issues that should be considered.

Sincerely,

J. Thomas Doman Chair,

Watershed Committee Member,

Board of Directors, PVCA

cc: Jeff Confer, Con-Stone, Inc.

Hon. Jake Corman, Pennsylvania Senate

Hon. Kerry Benninghoff, Pennsylvania

House of Representatives

Pennsylvania Trout Unlimited

In announcing its decision later, the agency says, "The many public comments the Department received regarding this application formed the basis for modifications to the permit revision and resulted in changes in [the mining company's] proposed mining plan." The bureau's decision is to allow deeper mining, but to require new modifications intended to protect groundwater conditions.

Example 4

This is a letter by a citizens group requesting the public meeting described in the scenario given earlier.

LETTER

July 16, 2001

Re: Application for amendment for Con-Stone mining permit #14920301, Aaronsburg Operation

District Mining Manager

Department of Environmental Protection

Bureau of Mining

Hawk Run District Office

PO Box 209 Hawk Run, PA 16840–0209

On behalf of the Aaronsburg Civic Club I am requesting a public conference on the proposed amendment to the above permit. Again this year, we are offering our facility, the Aaronsburg Civic Club Community Building, for that purpose. As you are aware last year's public meeting was well attended and provided an opportunity for residents to state their concerns and for Con-Stone and DEP to address them. This is as it should be in a free and democratic society.

I strongly urge you to hold a public meeting on the latest proposed permit revisions. Two concerns that have been brought to my attention are (1) the potential degradation of underground and surface water, and (2) mining on land previously designated for storage.

Please contact me to reserve our facility.

Sincerely yours,

Earl Weaver, President

Aaronsburg Civic Club

WHAT THESE EXAMPLES SHOW. All the examples in this chapter exhibit qualities of effective public policy communication (Checklists, Chapter 2). They illustrate useful public comments made from a variety of legitimate perspectives. They show a range of policy actors who exercise the right to comment on proposed government action. Taken together, the examples suggest the robust potential of the genre, formal public comment, for getting concerns onto the public agenda and into the public record.

Takeaway and Look Ahead

Democratic self-governance depends on citizens' willingness to intervene in the process. It is surprising that few of us comment on action that government intends to take when the responsible agencies directly ask us to do so. This chapter aims to encourage and enable the practice of formally commenting on proposed government action. Next, to conclude this guide, a code of ethics for public policy communicators is suggested.

For Discussion

Example 1, this chapter, illustrates public comment during 2014 rule making to revise the definition of "waters of the U.S." (WOTUS) in the Clean Water Rule for administration of the 1972 Clean Water Act. A new regulatory definition was codified in 2015; however, litigation delayed implementation. In February 2017 President Donald J. Trump ordered the responsible agencies to conduct new rule-making to review and rescind the 2015 definition of WOTUS.

To prepare for discussing this policy problem intelligently and critically, read EPA's arguments and language used to define "waters of the U.S." (https://epa.gov/wotus-rule). Then, discuss any of the following: your definition of "waters of the U.S." as a policy problem; your critical analysis of the language used in the discourse of federal water protection; other communication issues associated with clean water protection.

Exercises

Exercise 1: Comment on Waters of the U.S.
Draft a formal comment intended for submission to EPA regarding review of the 2015 Clean Water Rule. Write I, You, and It drafts (Exercise 1, Chapter 2) to clarify your position. Apply federal plain language guidelines to simplify your expression. Review tips for submitting effective comments (Task 2, "How to Write a Public Comment," this chapter) to assess the likelihood your comment will be taken seriously.

You will not actually submit the comment because the open public comment period ended in August 2017. However, keep it on file. You will be ready to submit it (adapted as needed) to a future call for comment. For now, the exercise of writing your own comment prepares you to critically read other comments submitted to Docket ID EPA-HQ-OW-2017-0203-0001 (http://regulations.gov).

Exercise 2: Comment on Clean Energy
"The Trump administration is moving to roll back the centerpiece of [the 2015 Clean Energy Plan] by easing restrictions on greenhouse gas emissions from coal-fired power plants. . . The EPA won't prescribe an immediate replacement to the plan, but will seek public comment on whether to curb climate-warming emissions from coal and natural gas power plants." (https://www.nytimes.com/aponline/2017/10/06/us/politics/ap-us-trump-climate-plan.html)

Apply this chapter's approach ("How To") to draft a formal comment on curbing air pollution from power plants. To know when to submit the comment, follow the news on national energy policy development. Watch the *Federal Register* or other sources for an EPA call for comments on the matter.

Reference

Bullock, D. (2014, March 12). Interview. Research Triangle Institute. Raleigh, North Carolina.

Federal plain language guidelines. https://www.plainlanguage.gov/guidelines/

"Public comments make a difference." http://regulations.gov/docs/Fact_Sheet/Public_Comments/Make_a_Difference.pdf

Schlosberg, D., Zavestoski, S., & Shulman, S. W. (2007). Democracy and e-rulemaking: Web-based technologies, participation, and the potential for deliberation. *Journal of Information Technology & Politics*, 4(1), 37–55.

Shulman, S. W., Schlosberg, D., Zavestoski, S., & Courard-Hauri, D. (2003). E-rulemaking: A social science agenda. *Social Science Computer Review*, 21(2), 162–178.

"How to use Regulations.gov" regulations.gov/help

CONCLUSION

Ethics for Policy Communicators

Overview

Ten chapters of this guide have taught efficient and useful communication. But efficiency and utility might not be enough. Communication ethics require attention, too.

* * *

During the 2016 national election and subsequent change of administration, American public policy communication culture changed in troubling ways. At the federal level, lack of verifiability ("alternative facts"), unreliability ("When can we believe what the president says?" asked a news reporter), and unaccountability ("When he's not kidding" answered the president's press secretary) became routine.

At all levels, political extremism, partisanship, elected officials' disregard for truth, and public hostility toward governance now make policy communication difficult in both obvious and subtle ways. Communicators find themselves reflecting on the why of their effort. They might question the morality of a particular choice or decision. So, guidance here concludes by suggesting practical ethics for policy communicators.

"Write to others as you would have others write to you. " (Williams & Colomb, p. 125). If this principle underlies all your communication, it might be all the guidance you need.

If you want more guidance, consider the following ethical principles and related practices. They are borrowed from codes of professional conduct in policy-interested fields and applied here to communication. An exercise invites you to make them part of your know-how.

Public Policy Communication Code of Ethics

Preamble
When communicating in a public policy process, I seek to serve the public good and to support good governance.

Principles
Judgment
I exercise my critical abilities to question the source, perspective, accuracy, reliability, timing, and potential consequences of information from any source. I abide by the same standards to which I hold others. I examine the values and circumstances that influence my communication choices. I am aware of and prepared to explain or justify my choices.

Honesty
To the best of my ability, I provide truthful and accurate communications. I exercise care to avoid error. I do not deliberately distort or mislead.

Understandability
I aim for conciseness, clarity, coherence, and contextual fit. I strive to address the interests and needs of those who use my communications.

Sensitivity
I recognize that my representations have consequences and can cause harm. I exercise my compassionate abilities to minimize adverse effects. I take care to avoid using positive or negative emotion or offensive comparisons to make a point. I respect all persons in their dealings with public institutions and organizations.

Civility
I observe civil and legal constraints on the use of information such as privacy rights, security controls, and confidentiality policies.

Practical Takeaways
Judgment

- Read critically. Ask who is presenting the communication; how it is framed and what the viewpoint is; what the message is; why it occurs at this time. Recognize its intentions, values, and assumptions. Identify techniques of representation, especially persuasive strategies—storyline, metaphor, analogy, synecdoche. Identify old information reused in a new context.
- Write intentionally. Know the values and assumptions underlying your choices of content and representation.
- Write appropriately. Know the circumstances in which your communications are, and are not, relevant in the situation.

Honesty

- Write verifiably. Check facts. Cite sources. Verify and critically consider sources before using them. Avoid lying. Avoid betraying readers' trust and confidence in your authority.

Understandability

- Write for readers. Attempt to know readers' situations, positions, information needs and uses. Anticipate the communication's intellectual and emotional impact on readers.

Civility

- Recognize and understand the constitutional, legislative and regulatory framework in which you work. Know how those frameworks affect your communications.
- Recognize and understand constitutional principles of equality, fairness, and due process. Be able to account for those principles in your communication practice.
- Exercise awareness of tone. Recognize information's emotional quality or attitude, implied or expressed. Anticipate effects of a communication's tone on readers' receptivity to and use of its information.

Sensitivity

- Exercise empathy. Be aware of a communication's potential effects, whether social, cultural, intellectual, or emotional.

- Exercise cultural awareness. Observe decorum and standards for public interaction. The default in any situation is politeness. Express concerns, opinion, and arguments politely.

Look Ahead

Can government function without a common or shared understanding of truth? Is American democratic governance harmed when public lying is normal? What do you think? Depending on your answer to that question, what are a public policy communicator's responsibilities for truth?

Exercise

Describe an Ethical Dilemma

Imagine that you are a communicator in a policy workplace. Imagine that you are asked to communicate information that you know is untrustworthy because it is false, taken out of context, or unverifiable. What are your choices in that situation? How will you decide what to do? What might you do? What might happen as a consequence? Write a scenario depicting this situation. This is a "think piece" for you, not for distribution. Perhaps use I, You, and It drafts to develop your thoughts (Exercise 1, Chapter 2). Use the ethical principles and practices summarized in this Conclusion as prompts.

References

American Political Science Association (2013). *A guide to professional ethics in political science,* 2nd ed. http://apsanet.org/portals/54/Files/Publications/APSAEthicsGuide2012.pdf

American Society for Public Administration (2013). *Code of ethics.* http://aspanet.org/ASPA/Code-of-Ethics

American Public Health Association (2002). *Principles of the ethical practice of public health.* https://apha.org/~/media/files/pdf/membergroups/ethics_brochure.ashx

American Psychological Association (2017). *Ethical principles of psychologists and code of conduct.* http://www.apa.org/ethics/code

Association of Government Financial Management Professionals (2017). *Code of ethics.* https://www.agacgfm.org/About/Code-of-Ethics.aspx

National Center for Civil Discourse (2017). *Second research convening summary.* http://nicd.arizona.edu/research-convenings

Public Relations Society of America (2000). *Member code of ethics.* https://www.prsa.org/ethics/code-of-ethics/

Society of Professional Journalists (2014). *SPJ code of ethics.* https://spj.org/ethicscode.asp

Society for Technical Communication (1998). *Ethical principles.* https://www.stc.org/about-stc/ethical-principles

Williams, J. M., & Colomb, G. G. (2012). *Style: The basics of clarity and grace* (4th ed.). Boston, MA: Pearson Longman

Writing Clearly

Clear sentence construction is here applied to the task of writing a policy memo. Tips by an experienced teacher of policy memo writing demonstrate a key principle of clarity, identifying the actor and the action. At the end, links are provided to online tools for assessing a document's use of plain language.

Tips on Writing a Policy Memo

By Peter J. Wilcoxen
Department of Public Administration and International Affairs
The Maxwell School, Syracuse University
Used by permission.

There's no single formula for writing an effective policy memo because every policy is different. However, here are a few guidelines that may help:

Be Concise

Remember that being concise does not just mean the memo should be short; it means that it should be no longer than necessary. Being concise does not mean leaving important things out; rather, it means don't write a paragraph when a sentence or two will do.

> *Bad:* "Some people will react to the increase in the gas tax by taking taxis, buses, or other public transportation since those forms of transportation are now somewhat less expensive than using a private automobile. However, some people may not be willing or able to make such a change: they might live far from public transportation or might have medical conditions that made it necessary

for them to drive. These people will continue driving but they would generally be likely to take fewer trips than before the tax."
Problem: Far too many words for the basic points being made!
Better: "A higher gas tax would reduce the amount of driving by people who can easily use other forms of transportation. People who can't switch would continue to drive, although they would probably drive fewer miles than before."

Briefly Explain Key Results
Don't ask people to take your results on faith. Briefly explain the key mechanisms and make clear how your analysis links to underlying data.

Bad: "The $7,500 tax credit will increase the number of electric vehicles sold by 75,000 per year."
Problem: The reader has to take your word for it with no supporting evidence: it's not clear what underlying data you used to reach the conclusion.
Better: "Survey X of vehicle manufactures (or whatever the source was) has shown that electric vehicle sales rise by 10,000 for every $1,000 reduction in price. As a result, the $7,500 credit could be expected to raise sales by 75,000 vehicles."

Don't Drag the Reader Through Step by Step Calculations
Although it's important to explain your results briefly, avoid going step by step through the calculations. The details can be put in a separate report to be circulated to people interested in the technical issues.

Bad: "To calculate the effect of the proposed $5 tax on each new tire sold, it is first necessary to convert the tax to an equivalent percentage change in the price. The average price of a tire is $100 so the tax would raise the price by 5%. Next, the percentage change in the price is multiplied by the price elasticity of demand for the good. The elasticity shows the percentage change in the quantity demanded for a percentage change in the good's price. Multiplying it by the price change thus shows the percentage change in the amount of the good that will be demanded. The demand elasticity for tires has been estimated to be in the range of -0.2 to -0.4. Thus, the 5% increase in tire prices would reduce tire sales by 1% to 2%."

Problem: The reader does not want to be taught how to do the calculation, she just wants to know the answer.
Better: "The tax would raise tire prices by 5%. Historically, tire sales fall by 2–4% for a 10% increase in price, so in this case it is likely that tire sales would fall by 1% to 2%."

The only time you'd need to put in much detail about the underlying calculations would be when there are multiple competing methods that give conflicting results. For example, suppose you needed to report the average number of cigarettes consumed by women between the ages of 19 and 25. It would be important for the reader to know whether the data was obtained by surveying women about their smoking habits or by observing the sales of cigarettes. People tend to underreport their consumption of cigarettes so survey data would be biased downward.

Identify the Winners and Losers

It's very important to figure out who would be helped and who would be hurt by a proposal. After all, the point of public policy is to solve public problems and thereby make people (at least some people) better off. No policy analysis is really complete until the winners and losers have been identified.

In addition, knowing who gains and loses can be very helpful in anticipating how the political process will play out. It will indicate which groups could be expected to support the policy and which groups would be likely to oppose it. Moreover, calculating compensating variations or changes in consumer and producer surplus will show how much it would cost to compensate the losers. To the extent that compensation can be built into the policy, political obstacles will be reduced.

Bad: "Eliminating rent control will benefit an average tenant by $75."
Problem: Too little detail; it sounds like everyone gains when really some tenants lose.
Better: "Eliminating rent control will cause rents to rise by $600 for 500 tenants currently in rent controlled apartments. However, it will also bring 300 new apartments on the market. The average value of each new apartment to its tenant will be $1,200 above the amount the tenant pays in rent."

Anticipate Questions

Look over your preliminary results and try to anticipate what questions a reader would be most likely to ask, or what additional calculations he might want to do to understand your results fully.

> *Bad:* "The policy reduces the average wages for entry level clerical workers from $6.00 per hour to $5.50 per hour."
>
> *Problem:* Virtually every reader will mentally convert this to a percentage to gauge how important it is.
>
> *Better:* "The policy reduces the average wages for entry level clerical workers from $6.00 to $5.50, a decline of 8.3%."

Don't Use Unnecessary Jargon

Avoiding jargon will make it easier for your results to be understood by a wide range of readers.

> *Bad:* "The income elasticity of medical care is 1.5 so a 20% increase in average household income would increase the consumption of medical care by 30%."
>
> *Problem:* Incomprehensible to anyone not thoroughly trained in economics.
>
> *Better:* "Statistical evidence shows that a 1% increase in household income leads to a 1.5% increase in expenditure on medical care. Since the proposed policy would raise household income by 20%, it should raise the demand for medical care by 30%."

Use Tables

A table can often be worth a thousand words. It's a much faster way to present a set of numbers than to include them in the text and it can be a lot easier for a reader to understand. That's especially true when you need to show results for different demographic groups.

Make sure the rows and columns of the table are labeled clearly and avoid including unimportant data.

> *Bad:* "The benefit of the food stamp program to eligible households having two children would be $5,000. These households have an average income of $15,000 so the benefit would be equivalent to a 33% increase in their income. Eligible households with three children would receive $6,000 in benefits and have an average

income of $17,000 (benefits are 35% of income). Households with four or more children have an average income of $18,000 and would receive $6,500 (36% of income). Households with one child would receive $4,000 and households with no children would receive $3,000. The average income of these two groups is $14,000 and $18,000 respectively."

Problem: Lots of information but it's tedious to read and it's hard for the reader to compare across groups.

Table I Benefits received by households with different numbers of children

Number of Children	Average Income	Food Stamp Benefit	Relative Gain
0	$18,000	$3,000	17%
1	$14,000	$4,000	29%
2	$15,000	$5,000	33%
3	$17,000	$6,000	35%
4	$18,000	$6,500	36%

Better: "Table 1 shows the food stamp benefits and average income for eligible households with different numbers of children. Also shown is the benefit as a percent of the household's income."

Write for an Intelligent Nonspecialist

You'll usually know more about the policy problem and the analytical methods you use than the reader of the memo. That makes it easy to inadvertently write the memo as though the reader were ignorant or stupid. The problem is subtle because it usually happens as a result of the best of intentions on your part: in trying to be as clear as possible you end up explaining things that the reader already knows or can easily figure out for herself.

Bad: "The policy will lower the price faced by consumers. When a good's price declines, consumers generally buy more of the good. Therefore, we would expect more units of the good to be sold."

Problem: It's both basic economics and common sense.

Better: "The policy will lower the price faced by consumers and thus increase total sales of the good."

Focus on Your Results, Not Your Opinions
Wherever possible, the memo should include all the facts a policy maker would need to reach her own conclusions and should not emphasize your personal opinion.

> *Bad:* "U.S. car manufacturers would gain by $1 billion per year if fuel economy standards were relaxed while U.S. consumers would not be hurt significantly."
> *Problem:* The reader doesn't know what you consider significant.
> *Better:* "U.S. car manufacturers would save $1 billion per year in costs if federal fuel economy standards were relaxed. The net effect on consumers is much smaller: the reduction in vehicle prices would save a typical household $200 but the drop in fuel economy would increase gas expenditure by $220."

(Please note: these figures were made up as an illustration and are not based on real facts about the U.S. automobile industry.)

Evaluate Means, Not Ends
Finally, focus on whether the policy is a good means for achieving its stated or implicit purpose, not whether the purpose itself is good or bad. For example, suppose Policy A intended to help Group X is grossly inefficient. The memo could argue that Policy A is a bad way to help Group X (i.e., that there are other policies that could achieve the same goal with less waste). However, it should avoid arguing that helping Group X is good or bad per se. That is, take it as given that Group X is to be helped and evaluate whether or not the policy is a good way of doing so.

> *Bad:* Policy A is worthwhile because it helps Group X.
> *Problem:* Helping Group X is the purpose of the policy so this is a statement about the goals of the policy, not about its means. It's not addressing whether or not Policy A is the best way to help Group X.
> *Better:* Policy A helps Group X but is much more expensive than delivering the same benefits via Policy B.

►▬• **WHAT THESE TIPS SHOW.** A key principle of clarity applies in each of these suggestions. The principle: identify the actor and the action. To tell readers clearly what you mean, build each sentence to show who (subject) is doing (verb) what.

Writing sentences (or rewriting them) in accordance with the actor-action principle would eliminate most of the problems in the examples shown here. Those problems are created by failure to focus on the main actor and action. To illustrate, look again at the bad sentence in the first tip, "Be Concise. " Keep the actor-action principle of clarity in mind as you look. In that bad sentence, the subject (italicized) is the grammatical subject but it is not the main actor. The verbs (underlined) show too many actions. The reader must guess which action matters most.

> *Bad:* "Some *people* will react to the increase in the gas tax by taking taxis, buses, or other public transportation since those forms of transportation are now somewhat less expensive than using a private automobile. However, some *people* may not be willing or able to make such a change: *they* might live far from public transportation or might have medical conditions that made it necessary for them to drive. These *people* will continue driving but *they* would generally be likely to take fewer trips than before the tax."

Now look at the better sentence with the principle of clarity in mind. The grammatical subjects (italicized) are now the main actors. The verbs (underlined) show only the most important actions by each actor.

> *Better:* "A higher gas *tax* would reduce the amount of driving by people who can easily use other forms of transportation. *People* who can't switch would continue to drive, although *they* would probably drive fewer miles than before."

Crafting clear sentences takes practice. Probably the best way to learn is by rewriting. "Most experienced writers get something down as fast as they can. Then as they rewrite that first draft into something clearer, they understand their ideas better. And when they understand their ideas better, they express them more clearly" (Williams & Colomb, p. 5).

Reference

Williams, J. M., & Colomb, G. G. (2012). *Style: The basics of clarity and grace* (4th ed.). Boston, MA: Pearson Longman.

Suggested Reading

If you want to explore this guide's concepts more fully, the sources referenced at the end of each chapter are recommended reading. Among those sources three are especially pertinent:

Deborah Stone (2012). *Policy paradox: The art of political decision making,* 3rd edition (New York: W. W. Norton).

David L. Helfert (2017). *Political communication in action: From theory to practice* (Boulder CO: Lynne Rienner Publishers).

Joseph M. Williams and G. Colomb (2012). *Basics of clarity and grace,* 4th ed. (Boston: Longman).

Williams and Colomb's *Basics* covers topics such as communicating complexity that are especially applicable to policy work. Abundant real-world examples are given, too. For these reasons, this source is preferable to William Strunk Jr. and E. B. White's *The Elements of Style.*

Good supplemental instruction on clear writing is offered in the regularly updated "Federal plain language guidelines" (http://PlainLanguage.gov).

Writing Public Policy: A Practical Guide to Communicating in the Policy Making Process is used in varied academic disciplines including public policy studies, political science, public administration, public health, policy writing, professional communication, and public affairs communication. Because it is widely used, no single discipline's readings are recommended beyond those cited in chapter references. That said, two sources are especially helpful to public policy students on a topic neglected by this guide, communicating results of quantitative analysis:

W. D. Coplin with E. Sandefer (2007). *The Maxwell manual for good citizenship: Public policy skills in action* (Lanham, MD: Rowman & Littlefield).

Irene S. Rubin (2016). *The politics of public budgeting,* 8th ed. (Washington DC: CQ Press).

Index